Talks given to Osho Commune International
in Gautama the Buddha Auditorium,
Poona, India, January 13 – 16, 1989

One Seed

🌱

Makes the Whole Earth Green

OSHO

Editing by Swami Anand Robin M.A. (Cantab.),
Typesetting by Ma Anand Disha
Design by Ma Krishna Gopa
Painting by Swami Shivananda
Photography by Swami Premgit,
Swami Puneet Bharti, Ma Deva Sarito
Production by Swami Prem Visarjan,
Ma Punyo
Printing by Mohndruck,
Gütersloh, West Germany

Published by The Rebel Publishing House GmbH,
Venloer Straße 5-7
5000 Cologne 1, West Germany;

1075 N.W. Murray Road
Suite 258
Portland, OR 97229, USA

Copyright © Neo-Sannyas International
First Edition
All rights reserved

No part of this book may be reproduced or transmitted in any form
or by any means electronic or mechanical including photocopying
or recording or by any information storage and retrieval system
without permission in writing from the publisher.

ISBN 3-89338-077-9

In loving gratitude to Osho
Rajneesh Foundation Australia

Contents

Peace of Mind,
My Foot!
page 1

The Secret
of Coca-Cola
page 41

1,758,670,175
Devils
page 83

One Wonders…
page 137

Introduction

THERE ARE VERY FEW OF US who still conceive of God as an old bearded figure in the heavens, watching and controlling everything like a celestial puppeteer. This seems to be for children or for fundamentalist believers of different religions.

And yet, as sophisticated as we think we are, we are still carrying remnants of this perfect, eternal authority figure. We have simply transferred it, in very subtle ways, to our governments, to our newspapers, to religious leaders, scholars, to people with titles and degrees after their names. We think that somehow they know something which we do not; that they have some truth which we are not aware of.

In these discourses, Osho shakes us to our very roots. He wants nothing more than to give us back to ourselves – not to accept anything on anyone's authority except our own. To read about a thirsty man drinking water will not quench our own thirst. Knowledge, scholarliness will only make us well-trained parrots; and unless something is from our own experience, it is simply not true.

Using *sutras* and anecdotes of Rinzai and other Zen masters as a springboard, this living Master shares His vision and His being with us. He invites us to inquire – not to accept, not to believe, not to take His word for it, but simply to inquire… "I want you to understand absolutely: never believe in anything. Experiment. Belief prevents you from searching for the truth. Never stop at a belief. Stop only at an experience of your own."

For Osho, Zen is the only true religion; the only approach to religion which has not put fetters on mankind, made sheep out of born lions. It is a seed, pregnant with vast potential, which can indeed make the whole earth green.

"...Zen is going to be paving the path for the new man to come, and for the new humanity to emerge. It is the only authentic gold that has come out of the whole past of humanity.

"My love for it is not in vain."

His words can give only a hint, but they contain His flavor. If we can just relax and read with open hearts, then the possibility is there for us, too, to discover that there is a fountain within us, a place to which each of us can return and quench our thirst.

Swami Geet Govind

Note to the Reader

THE END OF EACH DISCOURSE in this series follows a certain format which might be puzzling to the reader who has not been present at the event itself.

First is the time of Sardar Gurudayal Singh. "Sardarji" is a longtime disciple whose hearty and infectious laughter has resulted in the joke-telling time being named in his honor.

The jokes are followed by a meditation consisting of four parts. Each stage of the meditation is preceded by a signal from Osho to the drummer, Nivedano. This drumbeat is represented in the text as follows:

The first stage of the meditation is gibberish, which Osho has described as "cleansing your mind of all kinds of dust…speaking any language that you don't know… throwing all your craziness out." For several moments the hall goes completely mad, as thousands of people shout, scream, babble nonsense and wave their arms about.

The gibberish is represented in the text as follows:

The second stage is a period of silent sitting, of focusing the consciousness on the center, the point of witnessing.

The third stage is "let-go" – each person falls effortlessly to the ground, allowing the boundaries that keep them separate to dissolve.

A final drumbeat signals the assembly to return to a sitting position, as they are guided in making their experience of meditation more and more a part of everyday life. The participants are guided through each stage of the meditation by the words of the Master, and the entire text of each evening meditation is reproduced here.

Peace of Mind My Foot!

January 13, 1989

OUR BELOVED MASTER,
*One day, when Master Rinzai went to Ho-fu,
the governor asked him to take the high seat.
Then Ma-yu came forward and asked Rinzai,
"The great compassionate one has a thousand
hands and a thousand eyes.
Which is the true eye?"
Rinzai responded, "The great compassionate
one has a thousand hands and a thousand eyes.
Which is the true eye? Speak, speak!"
Ma-yu pulled the master down off the high seat
and sat on it himself.
Approaching him, Rinzai said,
"How do you do?"
Ma-yu hesitated.
Rinzai, in turn, pulled Ma-yu down off the high
seat and sat upon it himself.
Ma-yu went out, and Rinzai stepped down.*

Friends, the other day, the hilarious drama of a procession against me reached to the very peak. I have heard that three hundred donkeys surrounding one bodhisattva reached to the police commissioner's office asking for me to be arrested, because I am destroying the culture of a self-styled city which dreams of being cultured.

The one bodhisattva was carrying my effigy. The one bodhisattva looked like a donkey, and the three hundred donkeys looked like human beings. Even the donkey was laughing, because he was the only authentic being in that crowd: "What has happened to this cultured city and these so-called cultured people?"

Donkeys by their very nature are very silent people, very philosophical, very cultured. And this donkey was wondering, "Except me...all the three hundred donkeys who are hiding behind human masks, are doing *my* work, '*Cheepon, cheepon.*'" (*Hindi for* "Hee-haw, hee-haw.")

These so-called human beings, self-styled, cultured ones, thought that they were insulting me. Nobody in the world can insult me, because it is in my hands: if I accept the insult, it is okay; if I don't accept it, you have to carry it to your home. Nobody can humiliate me. Humiliation needs my acceptance.

On the contrary, these people were proving everything right that I have been saying to you. They were thinking that they are destroying my arguments by such processions. No procession can be an argument. No procession proves intelligence, it only proves retardedness. And carrying my effigy on a poor donkey simply exposes their real face: they are donkey-worshippers.

All human beings are not human beings. There are so many categories: a few are still chimpanzees, a few are still gorillas, a few are still monkeys, a few are still donkeys, a few are still yankees.

But in this so-called, self-styled cultured city, not a single person objected to these people, that "You are exposing yourselves, your vulgarity, your unculturedness."

And why are you harassing a bodhisattva? I call that donkey a bodhisattva.

And not only I, but since the day twenty-five centuries ago when Gautam Buddha gave Mahakashyapa a lotus flower, and told to the whole commune of ten thousand sannyasins, "What I could say to you I have said. What cannot be brought into language, I am transferring to Mahakashyapa. This lotus is just a symbol of transferring something which does not come into words."

And why to Mahakashyapa? – because he was the only one who had remained for years utterly silent. This day, when Buddha came for his morning discourse, everybody was puzzled. He had never carried anything in his hands, and today for the first time he was carrying a beautiful lotus flower. They were all waiting with excitement for what he was going to say, but he did not say anything. On the contrary, he simply went on gazing at the lotus flower for one and a half hours.

Everybody was puzzled, disappointed: "What is going on?" And at that moment, Mahakashyapa, after twenty years of silence, laughed so loudly.

At his laughter, Buddha called him close to him and gave him the lotus flower, and told the commune, "All that I could bring into words I have given to you. That which has remained beyond words, I am transferring to Mahakashyapa." That was the beginning of Zen. Mahakashyapa was the first patriarch of Zen.

Since that day, all these twenty-five centuries, hundreds of enlightened, awakened buddhas in the very thin stream of Zen have been asked again and again a question: Is the dog also a buddha? It can be changed to: Is the donkey also a buddha?

And all the masters in these twenty-five centuries have said, "Yes," without any hesitation. Every living being has the seed of the buddha. To have the seed of the buddha is expressed by the word 'bodhisattva'. Fundamentally, a buddha may have gone far away, may have become a donkey, may have become a dog. It does not matter. At the very center of his being he is carrying the seed. Someday, sometime, somewhere, the spring will come and the seed will start growing into a plant with foliage, and the seed will become a lotus flower.

So I say that, amongst these three hundred and one donkeys who had made a procession against me to the police commissioner, the three hundred were just phony human beings; only one was a bodhisattva – the donkey.

It was not an insult to be carried by a bodhisattva. I take it with great respect.

But these people are trying to prove me wrong, and they don't see that there is no connection: carrying my effigy…you can burn it, but why torture the poor bodhisattva, the donkey? Even that will not refute me.

I am going to take the issue of poverty.

All the religions are responsible for human poverty.

Jesus says, "Blessed are the poor, for they shall inherit the kingdom of God." Reading such statements, Karl Marx said that all these religions are nothing but opium to the people.

Jesus was consoling the poor: Don't be worried about your poverty, it is a test. Without complaint, patiently, just wait a little while, and you will be the inheritors of the kingdom of God. Just one life's poverty, and then an eternity of being a king in the kingdom of God. It is a good bargain.

And Jesus also said – just to console the poor so that they don't revolt against the rich, against the vested interests, against the exploiters and oppressors – he also said, "A camel can pass through the eye of a needle, but a rich man cannot pass through the gates of paradise."

It is not only Jesus, the same story is repeated in different forms, in different ways, to keep the poor poor.

In India it takes a different framework, but the conclusion is the same. All the three religions born in India don't agree on anything except this one point. You can understand why. They have their philosophies, mythologies, completely antagonistic to each other – Hinduism,

Buddhism, Jainism – but they all agree on one point: that the poor man is suffering because of his evil acts in the past life, and the rich man is rejoicing because of his good acts of his past life. They transfer the whole issue and misguide people.

You are exploited *right now,* and they are talking about past lives. It is not a coincidence that all the founders of these three religions had the patronage of the kings and the super-rich. Gautam Buddha was surrounded by kings and princes and the super-rich.

Who was there to give food and clothes and shelter to his ten thousand disciples? He moved with ten thousand disciples from one village to another village. The people were so poor, they could not afford food for themselves; how could they manage for ten thousand people?

But kings, super-rich people, followed the traveling caravan of Gautam Buddha, and provided them with shelter, provided them with food, provided them with clothes and every necessity that was needed. Why were they so much interested in Gautam Buddha? – because he was also saying that the poor are suffering from their evil acts in the past life.

It is very strange. The same is the logic of the Jainas, and the same is the logic of the Hindus: transfer the poverty to evil acts in the past. Nobody knows about the past; all that we know are the evil acts of the super-rich right now! They are exploiting in as many ways as possible.

You will not believe it, but even today in India there are five million human beings almost functioning as slaves. They are called bonded laborers. Rich people give them money in advance, and then they give them work, dangerous work in coal mines, in marble mines, and they are paid such a small amount of money per day that they are not able to repay the advance – and until they repay the advance they are bonded laborers. This is a very tricky phenomenon. Nobody sees it as slavery.

They have given one thousand rupees to a poor man so that he can make a hut, so he can get his daughter married, and then he has to work in a coal mine. Six rupees per day! – and he has to look after his whole family with six rupees. He will never be able to pay back that one-thousand-rupee advance, and until he pays that he has to remain in the coal mine.

People have suffered their whole lives in a strange, tricky slavery. Now, nobody can directly call them slaves, but the fact is they are bonded laborers; they will die, they will never get the money to pay the advance. The advance is given just the same way as in the past human beings were auctioned.

You will not believe that neither Buddha nor Mahavira nor Krishna nor Rama...nobody has said a single word against slavery. People, particularly women, were simply auctioned in the marketplace, and all these great religious leaders had nothing to say about it. Perhaps they are suffering from their evil acts of a past life.

And the most amazing fact is that not only did they not oppose it...

I am reminded of an Upanishadic Hindu seer – of course, self-styled and so-called – who was known as Gadiwan Raikva, because he used to travel in a bullock cart. Raikva was his name, *gadiwan* means a man who owns a bullock cart.

He was also in the marketplace bidding for a beautiful

woman, but a king came – and of course against the king he could not win. He went ahead as much as he could, because Hindu seers were not poor people; they had many wives, they had plenty of land, and their disciples worked on the land to pay for their discipleship. They gathered much money, and that money was used to purchase women.

Gadiwan Raikva was one of the most famous self-styled, so-called saints. What kind of saint is ready to purchase human beings as a commodity?

But because he was defeated and the king gave more money for the woman, he was very angry – and all these people have been saying, "Don't be angry, don't be greedy." He was waiting for his chance to take revenge – and these people have been talking about, "Drop all revengefulness, be kind, be compassionate, love your enemies."

After many years the king who had purchased the woman became fed up with his kingdom and riches and the whole crowd of women, and he wanted some peace of mind.

Forgetting the incident that had happened twenty years before, he went to Gadiwan Raikva to find some peace of mind, taking lots of money, diamonds, emeralds, rubies, to offer to the saint. He had taken with him his prime minister.

He touched the feet of Gadiwan Raikva and offered the whole lot of money. But Gadiwan Raikva was still boiling with rage. Twenty years had not made any difference, the fire was still alive. He pushed aside the king and said, "Get lost, and take all your money!"

The king could not believe it. He asked his prime minister, "What is the matter? Why is this man behaving so angrily? I used to think he was a great saint."

The prime minister said, "He is a great saint, but you don't remember.... Twenty years before you were both bidding for a young woman, and you defeated him. Bring that woman, offer that woman to the saint, and he will give you peace of mind." Peace of mind, my foot!

And he brought the woman, and Gadiwan Raikva accepted the woman, and he agreed to initiate the king into peace of mind.

A man who has been burning for twenty years with revenge, is he capable of offering peace of mind to anybody? He does not know anything about mind or peace!

These are the founders of religions. He is still respected by the Hindus.

All these three religions console the poor; that's why in India there has never been a revolution by the poor against the oppressors, exploiters. They take it as a matter of course that their poverty is because of their sins in the past, it has nothing to do with anybody else; there is no question of any revolution.

Mohammed said to his disciples – and they are still following his idea and being poor – he told his disciples one of the most absurd ideas: "You should not take interest on money, and you should not give interest on money."

Now the whole world of economics depends on interest. The more the money moves, the more money you have. That's why another name for money is currency: it has to be a current, continuously moving. But why should it move if I am not going to gain any interest on it? Why should I give it to anybody and take the risk? He may not return it.

So Mohammedans don't give interest on money, they don't take interest on money. Their whole economics is basically false, goes against the whole science of economics. The game of money depends on interest. Mohammedans have remained poor, utterly poor, and they are still following an out-of-date idea, thinking it is something spiritual.

All the religions are against money.

All the religions are praising the poor.

When you praise the poor, you are destroying all his possibilities of becoming rich. When you talk against money, you create a non-productive society. You can see it in India: five hundred million people are living in starvation at this very moment. And those who understand how an increasing population is going to create more poverty, they all predict unanimously that by the end of this century half the country will die because of starvation: one man amongst two. You will be surrounded in this country with corpses; you won't have enough wood for their funeral pyres, you will not have enough people to carry them to the graveyard. They will deteriorate, they will stink. The only people who will be happy will be the animals, the birds, who eat human flesh.

Amongst five hundred million corpses, do you think you will be able to live? I don't think any man of any intelligence is going to tolerate it. He would rather commit suicide, the scene will be so ghastly, so agonizing; such a tremendous anguish it will create.

But still the religious leaders are against birth control methods.

The pope comes to India and says to the poor people, "Using any birth control methods is against God." And the shankaracharyas, the heads of Hindu religion, talk in the same way. And the Jaina acharyas, who are the heads of the Jaina sects, are all against birth control methods. There is not a single religious leader who is in favor of birth control methods. These religious leaders will be responsible for the death of millions of people!

But why are they against birth control methods?

They say, "It is God who is giving you a child. To refuse it is against God." But to allow it to starve…? God seems to be a *monster*. He rejoices in children dying on the streets. He rejoices in the poor people who can't afford a single meal.

I have come across poor people who eat nothing but water. I cannot say they are drinking water, they *eat* water, and put on their stomach a brick to feel that their belly is full.

God loves these people…. God seems to be a greater devil than any other devil – and all these preachers, religious leaders, represent God. And they are all against humanity living in comfort, living an educated, cultured life, enjoying great paintings and literature and poetry and music and dance.

A hungry man cannot enjoy Beethoven.

A hungry man cannot enjoy Michelangelo or Leonardo da Vinci.

I am reminded of a great poet, Heinrich Heine. He got lost in a deep forest in Germany, where he had gone hunting. But he could not find his way out of the jungle for three days…and then came the night. Three days hungry…and he was afraid all the time of the wild animals, so in the nights he was sitting in the trees.

And then came the fullmoon night. He has written such beautiful poems about the full moon. No poet can afford not to write about the full moon; it has such a hypnotic power. It is the purest poetry.

Heinrich Heine has written many beautiful poems about the moon, but that night, after three days of hunger and tiredness and being afraid of death any moment, sitting in a tree he saw in the sky not a moon, but a loaf of bread. He could not believe his eyes. He rubbed his eyes, he looked again: it was a loaf of bread floating in the sky.

When he was found by a search party and brought back, he wrote in his diary, "Now I know how a poor man can enjoy the full moon, how a starving person can enjoy a lotus or a rose."

A poor hungry man has no time or mind to think about the greater mysteries of life; he thinks only of bread and butter. And God loves this drama...and the representatives of the gods are all in favor of poverty.

The world would have been finished with poverty long ago. It can still finish it! – but the religious leaders will not like it, because the religious leaders have power over the poor, not over the rich.

Who will give Mother Teresa a Nobel Prize if there are not orphans to be found on the streets in Calcutta? Just a one-day-old child, and the mother or the father has dropped it by the side of the road because they cannot manage its upbringing. And Mother Teresa and her seven hundred nuns are running around Calcutta, finding children who have been left by their mothers or fathers, and collecting them with great joy. Everybody is counting how many you have got. The joy is to convert them into Catholics.

Of course the pope is against birth control. If there

were birth control, there would be no Mother Teresa, and there would not be six hundred million Catholics. These are all the poorest of the poor.

In India I have been searching for thirty years for a single rich man who has been converted by the Catholic missionaries. I have not found one yet – but I have found that the people they have converted are the poorest of the poor. They don't understand a word about religion. They don't understand – they are not in a situation to understand. Mind needs a certain nourishment; they don't have that nourishment. And if somebody offers food and clothes and shelter, they are very willing to be called whatever you want: Catholics, Protestants, Christians – whatever you want.

Aboriginals, the primitive people who live in the forest almost naked – they don't have clothes, they eat the roots of the trees, they don't have food, and Christian missionaries are very happy to move into those parts and convert them to Christianity.

I was staying in the state of Bastar, which is inhabited by aboriginals, very primitive people but very simple and innocent.

The king of Bastar was my friend. Just because he was my friend, he was killed by the politicians – because he was supporting me in Bastar to help the poor people of his state to understand something about meditation. He had fallen in love with me, because he had learned meditation, and he wanted his poor people to learn meditation. So I used to go to Bastar…and to prevent me from going to Bastar, the king of Bastar was shot dead by the politicians.

I was staying in a small village where a missionary was managing to demonstrate to the aboriginals who is more powerful, Krishna or Jesus. I was sitting behind the crowd, so he would not recognize anybody from the contemporary world – and it was a dark night. He had a bonfire, and he set down a bucket of water and said to the people, who were very much excited to know who is more powerful...

He had made two statues, one of Krishna, made of wood.... No, the Jesus statue was made of wood, and Krishna's statue was made of steel! – but painted, they looked exactly the same. He took both the statues and put them into the bucket of water. Of course, Jesus remained swimming on top, Krishna drowned. People said, "Certainly Jesus seems to be more powerful than Krishna."

He said, "I have been telling you again and again that Jesus will save you, and Krishna will drown you, remember! Be converted to Catholics."

At that point, I could not resist. I stood up, and I said to the crowd, "It has been a very good experiment, but I want to ask you, have you ever heard of any test like a water test?"

They said, "We have never heard about it, but we have heard about the fire test."

So I said, "Now we should check both these fellows in the fire." And I told the people, "Catch hold of the missionary so he cannot escape," and I put both the statues in the bonfire, and Jesus burnt to ashes and Krishna came out.

They said, "My God! This man was deceiving us."

But this is the way they have been converting utterly primitive, poor people. And they want these people to be poor, otherwise they will not be able to convert them.

The Hindus have a difficulty: it is a non-converting religion just like the Jews. These are the two ancientmost religions of the world, and both are non-converting. You are born a Jew, never converted to be a Jew; you are born a Hindu, never converted to be a Hindu. Because these are the ancientmost religions, there was no need to convert anybody. Everybody was Hindu.

And more particularly, the Hindus have a caste system: the brahmins at the head, then the warriors, number two, then the business people, number three, and then the sudras – the poorest of the poor, the oppressed of the oppressed.

If you convert somebody, where will you put them, in which class? The brahmins will not allow anybody... Brahmins are born; it is their past lives together with austerities and purifications and discipline and virtue that has caused them to be born as brahmins. You cannot convert anybody to Brahmanism. Neither are the warriors, the *kshatriyas,* willing to accept anyone – they are high caste – nor the business people; they are the richest people. They don't want anybody to be converted, unnecessarily sharing their money.

The only class that remains is the sudras. But nobody would like to be converted to be a sudra, because they have a definite work to do: cleaning the Indian toilets, which are the *worst* toilets in the whole world, so primitive and ugly. And these sudras are carrying all kinds of shit on their heads! It is dropping on their faces!

Hindu society is immobile; nobody can move from his caste to another caste. The question of converting somebody from another religion does not arise. So it has been a good place to convert the sudras into Christianity.

I had a friend who was the principal of the greatest Christian theological college in the whole of Asia. Once or twice I went to visit him. I asked him, "Are you a born Christian?"

He said, "No, I am a born sudra," and he took me into his sitting room, and he brought an album to show me a picture of his father, who was a beggar. He and his children were converted to Christianity. The principal was educated, not only in India, but in Western countries. He showed me his picture before conversion and after conversion, and then he called his daughter.

I have come across millions of women, but she was a rare beauty, unbelievable. The grandfather, an ugly, starving beggar, and she was educated in America, had a doctorate, and was married to an American psychiatrist. They both used to come to India six months a year to convert poor people into Christianity, and six months they used to go to America to teach in the universities.

The old man, the principal, asked me, "What do you think?"

I said, "It is sheer exploitation of poverty. You are not converted on religious grounds; you are converted on financial grounds, and financial grounds cannot make a man religious. You are the head, the principal of the greatest theological college in Asia, and what is your work? – preparing missionaries to go around Asia to convert more poor people. None of these people…"

He had five thousand students in his college. He took me around. I said, "None of these people are convinced of the truth of your religion. You yourself are not."

He said, "I don't know anything about religion. All I know is about the scriptures, which I have been taught." And he took me to a class, which was so hilarious. This was the last postgraduate teaching for the missionaries, where they were taught how to speak, how to be great orators.

I watched for a few minutes; I could not resist laughing. I said, "This is such stupidity." They were being told when to speak loudly and when just to whisper, when to raise the hand, and when to beat on the table. I asked him, "Is this a college for actors? I thought you said to me it prepares missionaries. These are missionaries?"

When a man has something to say, then that very truth finds its way, its expression, its gesture. It has not to be taught.

But when you don't have anything to say, obviously you have to learn every gesture, every word. These actors are pretending to be missionaries; they will convert people to Christianity – and this they think one of the most virtuous acts. But for it they need poor people.

In the West, in the East, the framework may be different, but the outcome is the same. Don't allow the poor to rise upwards, keep them repressed, because they are the people to work and labor and do all kinds of things.

I have heard... A Rolls Royce stops before a hotel in Miami Beach. A woman comes out and shouts, "I need four persons to carry my son inside the hotel."

The son was not more than eight years old, but was really fat.

Four waiters came, and they said, "The boy looks so beautiful, can't he walk?"

The woman said, "I can afford for him to be carried by people. He does not need to walk! He's not crippled, he's rich."

On one hand, millions and millions are dying of starvation, and on the other hand, a few people have gathered all the money. Even their children have to be carried, because they can afford it. On one hand people are dying in the streets….

In the cold winter, three million Americans are living on the streets; nobody is going to take any care of them. And there are millions of people who do nothing; they simply sit before their television sets. The average time given to television in America is seven and a half hours per day. They cannot even move; they are so hypnotized by the television that now there are services from hotels available: they just have to phone for them to bring anything they want. These people go on becoming fatter and fatter…ice cream and Coca-Cola.

Now they have made a society – the society of the couch potatoes. They have become potatoes, they are no longer human beings.

You will not believe me, but there are people who cannot leave the television for any reason – even for making love. So they make love doggie-style, so both can watch the television!

This whole mess is created by your religions!

I blame everybody.

Moses destroyed the Jews by telling them a lie – that God has chosen them as his people. Because of this lie, the Jews have been tortured for four thousand years around the world, everywhere. Nobody can tolerate them, because they all think they are the chosen people.

Brahmins think they are the chosen people; God has written their scriptures himself. Mohammedans think they are the chosen people; God has sent his own *last* messenger with his message in the Koran. And, of course, Christians think God never sent to any other race in the whole world his only begotten son, Jesus Christ.

Everybody thinks... And Moses was the first to bring the lie, without knowing the implications. If you try to impose yourself as the chosen few of God, you will be destroyed, you will not be tolerated.

He went on Sinai mountain and after many days brought back ten commandments. Those ten commandments can be written on a small postcard. What was he doing for that long?

And if God was preparing the ten commandments on tiles of stone, could he, who created the whole world in six days, not create ten tiles in six days? Moses is lying; *he* was preparing those tiles, they are nothing to do with God. He deceived his people, just as all founders of religion are deceiving their people.

In the first place, God is a lie, the most fundamental lie. Out of the fundamental lie arise many lies. Lies don't believe in birth control either; they are very religious, they go on producing. One lie produces thousands of lies.

When God is accepted, how can you deny his only begotten son?

How can you deny his reincarnations in Rama and Krishna?

How can you deny his messenger, Mohammed?

Once you have accepted the fundamental lie, then you have to accept all these people, who seem to be a little bit insane. And these people have written your scriptures in the name of God – because the holy Koran is so faulty linguistically that it shows who has written it.

And if there is only one God, what is the need of so many religions, and so many scriptures, and so many prophets? Is it because God loves bloodshed, Mohammedans killing Hindus, Hindus killing Mohammedans? Just after India became independent, one million people were killed by Hindus and Mohammedans together, in the name of God.

An old Jew was dying. He had never gone to the synagogue. The rabbi came to tell him, "Now at least, make peace with God."

The old man said, "I have never quarreled with him in the first place. I have never gone to the synagogue, you know it well!"

The rabbi said, "You have always been strange. At this moment of death, pray to God!"

He said, "I am praying. I am praying that 'It is enough! We have been tortured enough because you have chosen us! Now choose somebody else!'"

Religions don't have any reason to exist in the world. Yes, religiousness is a totally different affair. One can be religious without belonging to a religion. In fact, those who belong to any religion cannot be religious. They can be Christian, they can be Jewish, they can be Hindu, they can be Buddhist, but *not* religious.

If you want to be religious, you have to stand on your own feet and look withinwards. God is nowhere outside. There is no person like God in existence. Inside you will find an eternity of consciousness. That is the only divineness, that is the only godliness – but there is no God.

To experience the godliness in your being will bring a great transformation, a metamorphosis. You will become a new man, with compassion, with love, with understanding, with intelligence, without any fear of death, because you know your eternity, because you know your very center.

A new series begins today: *One Seed Makes the Whole Earth Green.*

Maneesha has asked:

Our Beloved Master,
One day, when Master Rinzai went to Ho-fu, the governor asked him to take the high seat.

There have been men of intelligence even in such strange positions as governor. The governor asked Rinzai to take the high seat, higher than the governor. He knew.

Rinzai is one of the most beautiful masters. He had more enlightened disciples than any other master. His very air was that of enlightenment. His eyes were those of any awakened buddha. Those who had eyes to see and ears to hear, those who were sensitive enough to feel the fragrance of the man, immediately understood. He is in the crowd but not of the crowd. He looks just like a human being, but he has gone far beyond. He radiates his beyondness.

The governor must have been a man of great intelligence, understanding. He must have tasted something of meditation, otherwise it is impossible for a governor to tell somebody to take a higher seat.

Then Ma-yu came forward and asked Rinzai, "The great compassionate one has a thousand hands and a thousand eyes...."

This is just a metaphor for any awakened man. It simply means he can use his two eyes almost as if he has one thousand eyes.

You know my eyes: I have ten thousand eyes, and I look into every one of you. You may not know, you may not find it out, but I am watching continuously at the deepest core of your being.

It is a metaphor: the awakened one has one thousand hands. Can you see in my two hands, ten thousand hands?

The metaphor simply means that a master, just with two hands, manages to work almost as if he has a thousand hands. He works on thousands of disciples. He is the greatest creator in the world. He does not paint, he does not play the guitar, he does not sing. But what he creates is...he peels every disciple, uncovers the hidden treasure at the very center of every living being. His two hands are not just two hands, because he is working on thousands of people – hence the metaphor.

But there are idiots who will not understand metaphors, who will try to find out, "Is it true?" They want facts. As far as facts are concerned, Buddha has only two eyes and two hands, but as far as truth is concerned, he has ten thousand eyes and ten thousand hands.

To see what the tree contains one should look at the fruit of the tree; the fruit is decisive. If one awakened master creates a tremendous atmosphere in which unlit souls become afire, with his two hands he is doing miracles. With his two eyes he is looking in thousands of souls to awaken them. But it is a truth, it is not a factuality. You cannot take a photograph of it.

Ma-yu asked Rinzai,
"The great compassionate one has a thousand hands and a thousand eyes. Which is the true eye?"

"In one thousand eyes," he is asking, "which is the true eye?" He is behaving just like an average, blind, sleepy, unconscious human being, because those thousands of eyes are nothing but reflections of the one eye that is just in the middle of your two eyebrows. We have called it the third eye. These two eyes look outwards, that third eye looks inwards; that is the true eye. But that true eye can function on a thousand people, on ten thousand people, on ten million people.

The master never gives you any carbon copy; all are as authentic as the original. He always shares with you the original, the authentic. His clarity, his vision, is so vast that millions can share it. That is the meaning of the metaphor.

But the stupid persons would always ask questions about metaphors. They don't understand that there are things which cannot be said without metaphors – and those are the great things and great experiences in life, which cannot be expressed without metaphors, without poetry, without symbols.

Rinzai responded, "The great compassionate one has a thousand hands and a thousand eyes. Which is the true eye? Speak, speak!"

Perhaps you know; that's why you are asking.

It is one of the greatest fallacies with people who have accumulated some knowledge – all borrowed from scriptures, from teachers, from missionaries – all rubbish, because unless it is your experience, it is not true.

Rinzai must have looked into this man, Ma-yu. He seems to be a scholar who has been reading scriptures; hence the question. He already knows the answer – the answer from the scriptures, not the answer from his own experience. That's why he said,

"The great compassionate one has a thousand hands and a thousand eyes. Which is the true eye? Speak, speak!"

He wanted to expose Ma-yu: "Your knowledge is not your knowing. Your knowledge is all borrowed."

Don't depend on borrowed knowledge. That simply burdens you, makes you heavy, binds you into chains, imprisons you in words, and you forget completely your wings and the whole sky that is yours. But chained with religions and churches and scriptures, you cannot fly across the sun into the faraway blue sky; you cannot become one with the cosmos.

Ma-yu pulled the master down off the high seat and sat on it himself.

It is a very beautiful anecdote. Because Rinzai did not answer, and on the contrary started asking him,

"Which is the true eye? Speak, speak!"

he thought, "This fellow does not know even the scriptures. He is not a scholar." To show this, he pulled the master down off his high seat and sat on it himself. That's what scholars have been doing always.

Scholars are the arch enemies of those who have experienced the truth. That very experience of the truth makes the scholars feel so inferior that they become almost enraged. They lose all rationality and sensibility. They become insane.

Ma-yu pulled the master down off the high seat and sat on it himself.

Approaching him, Rinzai said, "How do you do?"

That's the beauty of a man who knows how to treat the idiots:

"How do you do?"

Ma-yu hesitated.

He could not understand what to say.

"How do you do?"

...and because of his hesitation he exposed himself.

The authentic master never hesitates. Hesitation comes out of doubt. Hesitation comes because you don't really know, you are only pretending. And just a small question – not a metaphysical or a philosophical question – just a simple question,

"How do you do?", and *Ma-yu hesitated.*

That was enough.

Rinzai, in turn, pulled Ma-yu down off the high seat and sat upon it himself.

Ma-yu went out, and Rinzai stepped down.

He was not interested in sitting on the high seat. He was interested in making Ma-yu understand that he does not know, but still he is pretending as if he knows.

All your scholars, all your preachers, all your so-called bishops and cardinals and imams and shankaracharyas are of the same category: they know much without knowing anything. They are very well trained parrots.

One bishop was very much in love with his parrot, but the parrot died. The beauty of the parrot was that he used to say the whole authorized Catholic prayer to God so phonetically, so accurately, that it amazed everybody who came to visit the bishop. But the parrot died.

It was a great despair how to find another such parrot, but he went to the pet shop and he told the sad story of his parrot dying. The shopkeeper said, "It will cost much, but I have the right parrot for you – far more refined than the one that has died."

The bishop said, "Money is not the problem. You just show me the parrot."

He took the bishop inside the shop, where he had put a parrot in a golden cage – a very beautiful specimen. The bishop asked, "What is so great about this parrot?"

He said, "You look closely. There are two threads hanging from his two feet. If you pull the right thread, he will immediately give the Sermon on the Mount."

The bishop said, "My God! And what about the left?"

"If you pull the left, he will recite what your parrot used to do. He will recite the Catholic authorized prayer to God."

The bishop was amazed, and he said, "If I pull both the threads together?"

The parrot said, "You idiot! I will fall on my asshole!"

Even parrots are far more intelligent than your so-called knowledgeable people.

Kikaku wrote:

A brilliant full moon!
On the matting of my floor
shadows of pines fall.

Always visualize these haikus.

A brilliant full moon! – and because of the brilliant full moon, *On the matting of my floor shadows of pines fall...* and a deep silence, and a tremendous blissfulness.

Those things are not said. They have to be understood by visualizing.

The next time there is a full moon, just watch the shadows of the trees falling on your floor. They don't disturb even a small particle of dust. They are there, but almost absent – just like the awakened being. He is here, but you can also say he is everywhere.

You can say about the awakened person that his presence and his absence are in equal parts – a higher mathematics for those who are searching for the highest pinnacle, the highest expression of their potentiality.

Neither does the moon want in any way to make shadows, nor are the pine trees interested in making shadows, nor is the matting of your floor interested in keeping those shadows. They come, they go, they move with the moon. Nobody is interested...but everything is happening so silently and so beautifully.

For a man who comes to his very being, life becomes just like that: everything happens so silently, so peacefully. There is not even a small disturbance in the dust.

Maneesha has asked a question:

Our Beloved Master,
I have understood that the witness is pure consciousness, unaffected by the body and mind it takes temporary residence in. So, first: How do personality traits and conditioning persist from one life to another?

And second: Does not that which makes us unique individuals have a continuum?

Maneesha, first you have to understand that you have not only this body of flesh and bones and blood, not only this brain which is part of the body. Behind the brain you have a mind – that mind is abstract – and behind the body you have an astral body. The word 'astral' comes from stars; it means a light…. Instead of flesh or bones, only a body made of light. This body of light, the astral body, has the mind in it.

When you die, your physical body and your physical mind are left behind. But the astral body travels with you, with the mind, with all the remembrances of the past life and the body, remembering all the scars and the wounds that have happened to the physical body. This abstract phenomenon travels with you; hiding within it is your ultimate, existential center.

Until you know the center, you will have to travel continuously from one body to another body. You have been traveling already for thousands of lives, gathering more and more memories in your astral mind, more and more memories in your astral body. Although your center is unaffected, it is surrounded by the astral body, and the astral body goes on from womb to womb, from grave to grave. That is your individuality; it has a continuum. But the continuum comes to an end when you become a buddha.

When you penetrate deeply to the center, you are also cutting the astral body apart, making a way through the mind, beyond the mind, through the astral body and beyond the astral body, to the center of your being. Once you have reached to the center of your being, the continuum of your individuality stops. Now begins the universal existence. You will not enter into another womb again, and you will not be burnt on another funeral pyre again. Now you will be one with the whole.

Of course, everything has a cost. You will have to drop your long-cherished love of individuality. Millions of years you have loved your individuality, but your individuality at the final stage is a hindrance.

Now take a jump out of the continuum and become one with the whole. You will disappear just like a dewdrop in the ocean. But it is the ultimate bliss, it is the most profound ecstasy to become the oceanic, to become the cosmic. You will never repent that you have lost your individuality.

What was in your individuality?

Have you ever thought?

Your individuality was a light prison, which carried you from one womb, passing through the grave, to another womb, and repeating the same things again and again and again. That's why in the East they call it the life and death cycle. To jump out of this cycle is the whole purpose of meditation – to come out of this continuum, which has been just a deep anguish, anxiety and angst, and to disappear into the blue sky.

This disappearance is not your death. This disappearance makes you one with the whole. And to be one with the whole is the greatest joy, the greatest blissfulness. Nothing is more significant, more full of splendor, more majestic. Here all the buddhas have disappeared in the ultimate eternity of existence. It is freedom from individuality, freedom from yourself.

You have known freedom from others, but you don't

recognize that you are still a slave of your own individuality. It is a cage…it may be golden.

Open the cage and fly across the sun into the blue sky and disappear, without leaving any footprints, any trace behind.

This Gautam the Buddha used to call *anatta,* no self, no mind, no you, no I. This in fact can be said in another way….

I have told you about Kabir, one of the great mystics of India. When he was young he became enlightened, and he wrote a small poem, in which comes the line: The drop has disappeared in the ocean.

When he was dying, he called his son Kamaal and told him to change that line. Kamaal said, "It is so beautiful – the dewdrop has disappeared in the ocean. Why are you changing it? And what is the substitute?"

Kabir said, "These are my last breaths; don't argue, simply do what I am saying. You write instead: The ocean has disappeared in the dewdrop. That was my first impression, this is my last impression." And he closed his eyes.

But both the impressions are beautiful. In the beginning, of course, you will see the dewdrop is disappearing in the ocean. But finally you will realize the ocean has disappeared in the dewdrop.

Now it is time for Sardar Gurudayal Singh.

Miss Goodbody says to her class one afternoon, "Okay, children, the one who gives me the right answer to the next question may go home right away."

ONE SEED MAKES THE WHOLE EARTH GREEN

Immediately, Little Albert throws his schoolbag out of the window.

"Who did that?" snaps Miss Goodbody, angrily.

"I did!" says Albert. "See you tomorrow!"

Paddy decides that it is time to get a full-time job. A new salami factory has opened in town, so he goes to apply. He picks up his application form, and he meets Mussolini McVey, the manager.

"Now, Mr. Murphy," says Mussolini, "we have got many applications for these jobs, so we have included two intelligence-testing questions. Come back tomorrow with your application and the answers to the questions."

At home, Paddy looks at the form.

Question 1 reads: How many seconds are there in a year? Question 2 reads: How many days of the week begin with the letter "T"?

The next morning, Paddy goes for his interview at the appointed time.

"Good morning, Mr. Murphy," says Mussolini McVey. "And what is your answer to the first question – How many seconds are there in a year?"

"No problem, sir," says Paddy. "The answer is twelve."

"Twelve?" asks Mussolini. "How did you get that?"

"Easy," replies Paddy. "The second of January…the second of February…!"

"Okay, okay Mr. Murphy," says McVey. "What about question two: How many days of the week begin with 'T'?"

"No problem, sir," says Paddy. "The answer is two."

"Very good," says McVey. "and by the way, what are they?"

"Easy," replies Paddy. "Today and tomorrow."

Farmer Scrumpy has been in the city for a couple of days, and when he gets back, Homer, his hired hand, collects him from the train station in the old farm Ford.

"How is everything, Homer?" asks Scrumpy.

"Ah, so-so," replies Homer.

"Anything much happen while I was gone?" asks Scrumpy, climbing into the car.

"Nothing much to speak of," replies Homer, driving off. "The dog limps a little."

"Really?" asks Scrumpy.

"Yup," says Homer.

"How did that happen?" asks Scrumpy.

"Well," explains Homer, "I guess the old horse was acting kind of crazy, running out of the stable, half scorched, in the middle of the night, and kicked him."

"The horse?" cries Scrumpy. "Half scorched?"

"Yup," explains Homer. "When the barn burnt down and all the hay went up in smoke, the horse got scorched."

"Really?" cries Scrumpy. "The barn burnt down?"

"Yup," replies Homer. "I guess a few sparks must have jumped from the house to start it. I got out of the house just in time."

"Really?" cries Scrumpy. "The house was on fire? How did you get out?"

"Well," explains Homer, "your wife kicked me out of bed and woke me up!"

"Really?" shouts Scrumpy. "You were in bed with my wife?"

"Yup! We were drinking your homemade whiskey."

"Really?" shouts Scrumpy. "You were drinking my whiskey and in my bed with my wife? Where is she now?"

"Well," explains Homer, "she got crisped in the fire, but don't worry! I saved the whiskey!"

"Thank God!" cries Scrumpy. "Did anything else happen?"

"Nope," explains Homer, "it was a pretty quiet weekend!"

Nivedano...

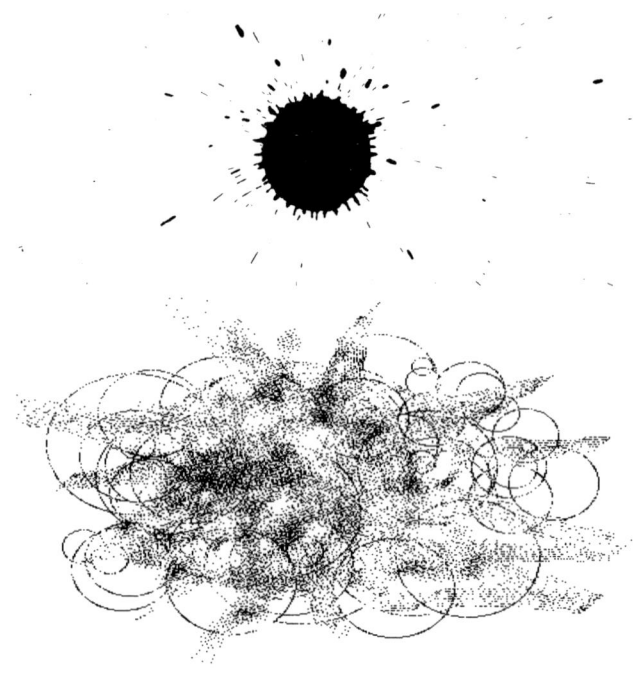

Nivedano...

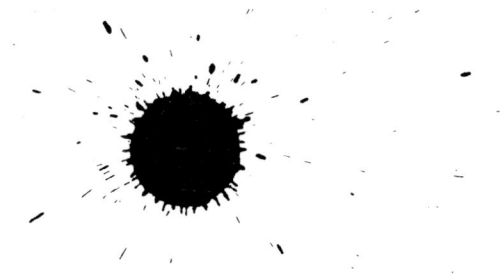

Be silent...
Close your eyes...
Feel your body to be completely frozen.

This is the right moment to look inwards, with your total consciousness, with your total life energy, and with an urgency as if this is your last moment on the earth.

Go deeper and deeper, penetrating every layer.

As you go deeper, you will find deep silence descending on you.

Deeper...a great peace that passeth understanding.

Still more, deeper...and flowers start showering on you with a fragrance you have never known.

At the very center of your being you will find yourself – not the way you have known up to now, but in a totally new way. You will find yourself one of the buddhas, alert, awakened.

And the buddha has only one quality: witnessing.

Now witness: the body is not you, the mind is not you – even the astral body is not you. Neither the silence, the peace, nor the fragrances are you. They are all around you, but you are only a witness.

Your only quality that is eternal is witnessing.

To make it clear, Nivedano…

Relax…

Let go, but remain a witness, remain a buddha.

This moment, you are the most blessed people on the earth. Ten thousand buddhas are melting, dissolving, and the Buddha Auditorium has become an ocean of consciousness.

Drink as much from this divine juice as possible, and persuade the buddha to come with you. He has been hiding in you for thousands of lives. Tell him to come out to the periphery, to the circumference of your life. Carrying water from the well, chopping wood, buddha has to be present every moment – waking or sleeping.

The day your circumference and center become one will be the greatest day of your life. The continuum of your birth and death will disappear. You will be enlightened.

And when you will drop this body, this mind…with this body and this mind you will also drop your astral bodies, your inner mind. You will become just a dewdrop – either disappearing in the ocean, or the ocean disappearing in the dewdrop. This is the ultimate peak of human evolution. The whole existence is waiting for it.

Whenever one man becomes one with the whole, the

whole existence dances, sings, showers flowers, celebrates.

Gather as much as you can before Nivedano calls you back. Persuade the buddha…. It is your innermost core, it is nobody else's monopoly. Hold his hand, show him the way, the golden path that you have traveled to the center.

Now don't come alone. Come with the buddha following you. He has to become your everyday life, your breathing, your heartbeat. He has to sing with you, he has to dance with you.

His being with you all the time will make your life a continuous festival.

Nivedano…

Come…but don't come alone.

Come as a buddha: peacefully, silent, with great grace.

Sit for a few minutes just to remember where you have been, just to remind you of your inner splendor, the great silence you encountered, and the buddha who has come as a shadow behind you. Each day he is coming closer and closer to you.

The day you and the buddha dissolve into each other, you are awakened, you are enlightened.

This is true religion.

This is authentic spirituality.

It does not depend on any organization or church. It is absolutely your journey towards your home. It is remembering a forgotten language.

And if one man can become a buddha, it is a proof that every man can become a buddha.

One seed makes the whole earth green.

Okay, Maneesha?
Yes, Beloved Master.

The Secret of Coca-Cola

January 14, 1989

Our Beloved Master,
Sanshō, a disciple of Rinzai, once said to Seppō,
"The golden carp is out of the net!
Tell me, what will it feed on?"
Seppō said, "When you have got out of the net,
I will tell you."
Sanshō said, "The renowned teacher
of fifteen hundred monks cannot find
even one word to say about this topic."
Seppō said, "I am the chief abbot
and have much to attend to."
On another occasion, some time later, Sanshō said
to a monk, "Where have you just come from?"
The monk said, "Kwatz!"
Sanshō said, "Kwatz!"
The monk again said, "Kwatz!"
Sanshō said, "Kwatz!"
The monk said, "If you strike me blindly,

I shall say 'Kwatz!'"
Sanshō picked up his staff, and the monk put himself in
readiness to receive a hit. Sanshō said, "When you go
down a slope, there's no pleasure unless you run down it,"
at which he struck the monk.
The monk said, "You robber!" and went off.
Another monk present at the scene asked,
"The monk just now – how can he enter?"
Sanshō commented, "That chap had been to see the
former teacher."

FRIENDS, I HAVE HEARD ABOUT an editor who was bitten by a mad dog. When he reached the hospital the doctor said, "It is too late, you are going to be mad."

The editor just said, "Bring me a paper and a fountain pen immediately."

The doctor said, "There is no hurry to make your will."

He said, "Who is making a will? I want to write the

names of the people whom I am going to bite when I become mad!"

I have been searching for this editor, and I have found him. He works here in this self-styled cultured city, in a daily newspaper, *Prabhat*. He has been writing in editorials absolute nonsense about me.

Before I answer him, I want to thank him, because anybody who writes any nonsense about me simply gives me an occasion, an opportunity to expose this self-styled religiousness, this so-called culture, utterly rotten. Before I answer him, I would tell you one thing more.

The editor did not die. On the contrary, the dog who had bitten him died. There are a few people so poisonous that if a snake bites them, the snake dies.

He is trying in every way to bite me, but I am not so available, so the poor fellow goes on writing editorials. I would love him to continue. I am absolutely grateful to him, for the simple reason that he gives me an occasion to expose this rotten society and its religion and its culture.

He has written about me that I am a "lecherous professor polluting the social and cultural climate." Okay…

This editor should remember that *I* have not made the statues of Khajuraho; they are one thousand years old. I have not made the sensuous, utterly obscene statues of Puri or Konarak. These statues of naked women in perverted postures in thousands of numbers…it must have taken hundreds of years for the sculptors to make these temples. And these statues are not just pure works of art, they are part of religion; otherwise why put them in the temples?

India has known the first lecherous man in Vatsyayana.

Three thousand years before Sigmund Freud and Havelock Ellis, he wrote the first book in the world of sexology, *Kamasutra,* aphorisms on sex. Hindus have been calling him maharishi, the great seer. His sutras are so ugly and obscene. He has also a few sketches of sexual postures. Those sketches are so obscene, so ugly, so unnatural – and you will not believe that he describes eighty-four postures of making love. You know only one posture: that is the missionary posture.

This man is not called lecherous, he is called the great seer. And this man for three thousand years has never been criticized by anyone; they have worshipped the man. And this poor editor calls me lecherous....

All the scriptures of the Hindus are full of lechery, full of obscene sensuality. I will describe the milestones.

The second man is a Kashmiri brahmin who wrote the *Kok-shastra.* Koka is his name, Pandit Koka. His sketches are far more ugly than Vatsyayana's *Kamasutras,* and he used to have a love affair with a woman of the lowest caste, the *kolas;* they are the aboriginals.

Sometimes I wonder... Joining 'koka' and 'kola', perhaps the secret of Coca-Cola is there! That's why the manufacturers of Coca-Cola don't allow the secret to be known by anybody.

And this poor fellow calls me lecherous, and Koka is called a great scholar, a great researcher in sexology!

In one of the Hindu scriptures you will see the whole scene, what it means to be lecherous.

You have seen the *shivalingas* all over India. Perhaps there are more shivalingas than anybody else's statues – shivalinga simply means Shiva's sexual machinery, and it is based in the *yoni* of Parvati, his wife – and openly, on the street corners, in the marketplaces. Shivalinga does not need even a temple, not necessarily. Even the poorest can afford it. Just find a piece of marble looking like a phallic symbol and make in the marble the vagina of a woman. Place the phallic symbol in the vagina and you have got the Hindus' *mahadeva,* the great god.

How did it come to happen that no other god has such symbols? I would like to tell you the story to explain the word 'lecherous'.

Just as the Christians have the trinity, the Hindus have *trimurti* – the three faces of God. The first face is Brahma, who created the world. He has only one temple in the whole of India, because who cares about him? – he has already done his job, and nobody knows where he has gone.

The second face of God is Vishnu, who has thousands of temples, because his work is to maintain what Brahma has created. Of course, if you can persuade him by your prayers and rituals, it will be a great blessing to you. He is constantly maintaining the universe till the moment when Shiva destroys it. Shiva is God the destroyer.

How did it come to happen that Shiva has got just a phallic symbol to represent him?

One morning, Brahma and Vishnu were arguing about something, and they could not come to a conclusion, so they thought, "It is better to go to Shiva. Perhaps he can help us to come to a conclusion." So they went to Shiva early in the morning.

Americans should not think that only they make love in the morning. Millions of years before, Shiva was making love to Parvati in the morning – with the door open.

Brahma and Vishnu never thought that this is the time

to make love – but Shiva is a very strange god, a hippy god. He takes marijuana, he takes opium, he drinks alcohol. There is not a single drug that he is not addicted to. Naturally, he has no sense of time, whether it is night or day, or whether the door is open or closed.

So Brahma and Vishnu entered and they could not believe their eyes. I call these fellows lecherous. If they had any gentlemanliness they should have gone out of the house, but they remained there for six hours, because that drug addict, Shiva, went on and on and on, not knowing when to stop. He did not bother that these two fellows were going around, watching what he was doing. These are the lecherous gods of the Hindus!

And when after six hours he came to his senses and recognized these two fellows, they cursed him. They should have cursed themselves, because they had entered into somebody's privacy. Seeing that he was making love, they should have gone out and waited outside. But they went round and round, watching and enjoying: this is lechery. You will not find another example of such divine lechery.

They should have cursed themselves, but rather than cursing themselves, they cursed Shiva – "because we were standing here for six hours, and you did not take any notice of us, and you went on making love. It is so uncultured that we curse you, that you will be known in the world only by your genitals." That's the reason for that shivalinga you see all around the country.

Now, I would like the editor of *Prabhat* to answer me: Who is lecherous? Your gods…?

And then I come to the father of this nation, Mahatma Gandhi.

ONE SEED MAKES THE WHOLE EARTH GREEN

While his wife, Kasturba, was alive... Her grave is just beyond the river in the Aga Khan palace; she died here in the custody of the British Empire. Mahatma Gandhi was also under house arrest in the Aga Khan palace.

Kasturba was very jealous of Gandhi, because he was mixing with so many people, men and women. She kept a constant vigilance.

Once India's great poet, Rabindranath Tagore, was staying in Gandhi's ashram, and Gandhi wanted to discuss many things with him, so he said, "It will be good if we sleep in the same room." Kasturba freaked out. She did not allow them to stay in one room.

So while Kasturba was alive, Gandhi was talking about *brahmacharya,* celibacy. In fact, everybody wants to be celibate as far as his wife is concerned. He wrote a book saying that celibacy is the true life, but it was just the fear of Kasturba and nothing else.

When Kasturba died, he started sleeping with naked women. All his followers have been trying to hide the fact, because they were worried that his image of the father of the nation would fall down into the mud. And unfortunately the three persons who were constantly harassing him not to do this were all from Maharashtra.

One was Kaka Kalelkar, a long-time, lifelong friend of Mahatma Gandhi. The second was Vinoba Bhave, one of the most intimate followers of Mahatma Gandhi. And the third was Dada Dharmadhikari, a man who has been trying to philosophize Mahatma Gandhi's ordinary statements. All three belonged to Maharashtra, the self-styled cultured and religious society.

But Mahatma Gandhi did not listen to anyone.

Because of his constant repression that he had been

calling celibacy...even after fathering five sons he was repressing his sexuality, sensuality, and only repressed people become lecherous.

Once his wife was dead, he forgot all about brahmacharya, celibacy, and started in his old age, at the age of seventy, having sexual dreams. And he is called the mahatma, the great soul – and he started at the age of seventy sleeping with naked young girls, and the whole of his following was trying to hide the fact.

But they could not hide it for a simple reason. Mahatma Gandhi's secretary, Pyarelal, was one of the most efficient secretaries one can have. But because he fell in love with a woman, Gandhi kicked him out of the ashram. In Gandhi's ashram nobody can fall in love; that is the greatest sin.

Pyarelal was writing a biography of Gandhi. He knew all the secrets – his sleeping with naked girls – and because he was kicked out of the ashram he may have had some revenge also in his mind. "The man talks about celibacy to the public, and from the backdoor he sleeps with young girls, and the girls have to be naked."

He wrote the biography, and it is such a big volume, with such accuracy of evidence – almost two thousand pages, two volumes, so it is beyond the reach of the ordinary public. Who is going to read two thousand pages? And the sleeping with the naked girls comes in the last one hundred pages, with all the details – who the girls were, with all the letters that he received from Kaka Kalelkar, Vinoba Bhave, Dada Dharmadhikari, persuading him to stop this practice: "This may destroy your image."

But it was the last period of his life, and what he had

repressed for forty or fifty years had become a volcano. It was beyond his control.

And this man, utterly immature, ignorant, calls *me* lecherous!

Call Mahatma Gandhi lecherous!

Call Brahma and Vishnu lecherous. Call Shiva lecherous – the first hippy of the world!

But this is the situation with all the religions. Hinduism is not an exception.

Five hundred pages in the Old Testament of the Bible are absolutely obscene. One friend of mine has taken out all the five hundred pages and made a new book, *The X-Rated Holy Bible.* Now the Christians are after him. But the book has gone ahead – although banned by many countries, it has reached an underground market.

Five hundred pages? And no Jew, no Christian – because both believe in the Old Testament – has ever objected? Call these people lecherous. And these were the prophets who have been writing all these things.

I am determined to expose everything, without holding anything back. So it is perfectly good that these people should continue to write against me. That will give me material, subject matter. Soon they will realize they are cutting their own heads.

I am not a man who can be suppressed by just calling me names. Criticize what I am saying, look at your face in the mirror, and find the passages in your own scriptures. You will find much more, because I am only giving samples to my people.

Another Marathi newspaper editor has asked me that,

"How can two souls live in one body?" – as if he understands what a soul is!

The soul is pure light, and in a room you can have one candle, you can have one thousand candles, because the light does not take space. The light is not the thing that takes the space. You can have one thousand... You can see around you thousands of bulbs and thousands of lights. The lights are not struggling for space, for territory. Light is not a space thing – and the soul consists only of the purest light, which does not need any fuel. So there is no question...

The editor has asked if I can prove this.

It is an already proved fact; I don't have to prove it.

All over the world people know it already, that a man can be possessed by spirits – and not only one. The highest count has been sixteen, sixteen souls possessing one man's body.

And if you want more data and research on the subject, you should go to Rajasthan, to Jaipur, to have a look in the University of Rajasthan – that is the only university in India which has a department for parapsychology. They have been collecting all the cases of possession by spirits – so you will know that it is not a question at all of space. Two souls can be in one body without any difficulty. They don't have any conflict of territory.

Just watch light and you will understand. One candle or one thousand candles in a small room – do you think there will be great chaos? One thousand candles? – where will they find the space?

Light does not need space.

I am answering this question, not for your sake, Mr. Editor, I am answering this question for my people to understand that the soul is pure light. That's why it has no weight, it does not occupy space. It has no limit as far as time is concerned.

Hundreds of experiments have been done around the world by the scientists. In one experiment in Germany, they put a man who was just on the verge of death in a box made of absolutely transparent glass, so they could watch him while he was alive, from the outside. The box was completely sealed. They wanted to know that, if the soul leaves the body, how can it leave the box? "We will catch hold of the soul." And if the soul leaves the body, the body must lose some weight, so they weighed the body as accurately as possible.

But the man died, and nothing left the glass box, because for the soul, matter is not a hindrance.

You know that x-rays can enter your body and the body cannot prevent them; you don't feel even that the x-rays are entering in your body when an x-ray is taken. The soul is a far more refined, ultimate light, so when it leaves the body you cannot see it. If you have not seen it already within yourself, you will never be able to see anybody's soul leaving him.

Then they opened the case, and they could not find it. So they weighed the dead man again: he had the same weight. For the materialist it is enough proof that there is no soul, because nothing has left the box and the man's dead body weighs the same as when he was living. For the materialist scientists it was enough to prove that there is no soul.

It is not enough for me.

The soul does not have weight.

Do you think light has weight? Try…put one candle on

your weighing machine, unlit. Weigh it, then give light to the candle and see whether it weighs more. There is no need to go to such lengths as finding a dying man; you can just try to weigh the light. It has no weight, but it does not prove that there is no light. It simply proves that light belongs to a different category. It is not a thing, hence it has no weight.

When you blow out a candle, do you see where the flame is going, finding the door outside into the street? You don't see anything. The flame simply disappears into the universe, leaving no trace behind.

The same is true about the soul.

And the first editor continues that I am "polluting the social and cultural climate."

What social and cultural climate have you got?

It was a man from this social and cultural atmosphere who killed Mahatma Gandhi – the first murder of its kind in this country. It is perfectly okay in America, but not in India.

In America, twenty percent of the presidents have been murdered – that is routine – but Mahatma Gandhi's murder was the first of its kind in this country. And the man who murdered him belonged to this cultural, social society. He was a citizen of this city.

An attempt has been made on *my* life in *this* city, by throwing a knife to kill me! I was informed by the police headquarters, before the morning discourse, that "We have received an anonymous phone call that somebody is going to throw a knife at you and kill you, so allow in twenty high-ranking police officers."

But the whole thing was totally different; it came

ONE SEED MAKES THE WHOLE EARTH GREEN

finally to a very different conclusion. Those twenty police officers were sitting behind the man who had thrown the knife at me. They immediately surrounded him, in order to arrest him.

Unfortunately for the poor man, he was not an archer, or a man who could manage to hit the target. The knife fell almost six feet away from me. What a great man they had found to kill me! If they had told me, I would have sat six feet away from myself!

They did not allow my people to bring a case. Ten thousand sannyasins were present here, eyewitnesses; you could not find so many eyewitnesses for any murder, or any attempted murder anywhere else. But the police officer said, "We are present, we will take the case to the court ourselves. It is a police case. You don't need to bother at all." That was the strategy.

They took away the knife also, saying, "We have to present it to the magistrate." The knife was never presented, and the magistrate simply dismissed the case: "There is no case. Where is the evidence?" And those twenty police officers remained silent.

It was a good conspiracy between the magistrate and the police officers and the cultured citizens of this city.

How am I polluting the social and cultural climate? I don't enter in your city at all; it is too polluted for me. It is the most polluted city in the whole of Asia, and soon it will be the most polluted city in the whole world.

I talk to my people; I never see the editors of *Prabhat*, and editors of other Marathi daily papers, weekly papers, monthly magazines. I don't see people from the city here. My people belong to the whole globe, and those few people from the city who are here, they have been with me for twenty years. They are now beyond any cure. I have corrupted them so much that now there is no medicine, no deprogramming that can bring them back to the normal lunacy of this city.

Just by the way, I would like to tell you a very beautiful case of a great evangelist who had millions of listeners on the radio, and watchers on the television.

In America, a new phenomenon is growing: TV evangelism. What is the need to go to the people? You just give the sermon in the television studio and it reaches to millions of homes.

This man, television evangelist Jim Bakker, has returned to American TV again. Where had he gone and why? He had admitted to having sexual intercourse with his secretary and homosexual relations with a male preacher.

This happened a few months ago. Then he went into seclusion just to avoid the public – because he was a great preacher, and they thought that God speaks through him. But when they found that he was having intercourse with his secretary, and is not only heterosexual, he is perverted – he was having a relationship with a male preacher... And on the television he was talking to everybody about the greatness of celibacy.

These are the people who really destroy humanity and its trust.

Now he is coming back. What excuse has he found? – a great excuse, but it won't do as far as I am concerned.

Now he is saying that the devil made him do it. He was a representative of God, and God even did not care to interfere. And it was not only one time, but for years the devil was telling him to do it, to make love to the secretary, to have homosexual relations with the preacher; it was the devil.

What was God doing? If he cannot save his own preachers, do you think he will save you? The devil seems to be more powerful.

He said, "The devil was jealous because I was forming a new church."

But what about God? You were making a new church for God.... God seems to be absolutely impotent; the devil was directing you for years. And you had been preaching about celibacy.... You could not say to the people, "The devil has been forcing me to do things which I don't want to do." You were found red-handed making love to the secretary, and there was no devil present who was forcing you, on the point of a gun, to make love. You could have at least reported to the police station.

It is not a coincidence that devil-worship is growing all over the world, particularly in Christian countries. In England, there are now thousands and thousands of people who worship the devil. In Australia, thousands of people worship the devil. And these devil-worshippers are Christians who have seen that God is impotent; the devil is a far more powerful being. Obviously, everybody wants to be on the side of the victorious.

These Christians are throwing stones at churches, throwing stones at Christian preachers, saying "You are misleading people. You are telling people that God will save you. God cannot do anything! The devil is more powerful."

It was the devil to whom Adam and Eve listened, not to God. God behaved like a self-styled, cultured Poona-ite.

Rather than persuading them, or going with them, the way the devil had argued, God had told Adam and Eve that they should not eat the fruits from two trees: one was the tree of wisdom, and the other was the tree of eternal life.

I cannot in any way... I have tried in thousands of ways somehow to see the point. A father is preventing his own creation from being wise, from having eternal life? What kind of father...? He must be counted as the greatest enemy, the archenemy of humanity.

It was the devil who argued with Eve. He said, "Do you understand why God has prevented you from eating from these two trees? It is because he is very jealous. He is afraid if you eat from these two trees you will be a god yourself. He does not want you to be a god, he wants you to live naked like animals in the forest." And he said, "If you don't believe me, you just eat and see."

Eve could see the argument clearly. If the father loved you, he would have insisted, "Eat more of the tree of wisdom and of the tree of eternal life, so that you will soon be grown up, so that you will soon realize your godliness." That would have been compassion, love. This is simply cruelty, violence, evil.

The devil was the first revolutionary friend of humanity. And when Eve ate the fruit, her eyes opened. She saw a totally different world. She ran to Adam and told him to eat the fruit. They were caught red-handed by God. Rather than giving any argument against the devil, he behaved just like an idiot. He drove them away, out of paradise.

In a small school a teacher was telling the story, and

she asked, "Can you say something about the story?"

One small boy, Albert, stood up, and he said, "As far as I can understand, he must have driven them in an old Ford car." Driving them out of paradise…what kind of car was he using? It must have been a Model-T Ford car, the oldest, the ancientmost.

The teacher was aghast. She said, "I had never mentioned a car."

Albert said, "You said he drove them out…"

This is ugly behavior on the part of God.

Telling them, "You have committed the greatest sin…"

Wisdom is sin? – then ignorance must be a virtue. Searching for eternal life is sin? Then committing suicide must be a virtue.

Adam and Eve could not reach to the other tree. Since then man has been searching for eternal life. Have you ever realized what you are searching for?

You are searching for more wisdom – enlightenment. You are searching for eternal life – a force which has no beginning and no end.

I cannot say anything against the devil worshippers. They are doing the right thing. It is perfectly good if devil worshippers and god worshippers fight and destroy each other. It will be a great blessing to humanity. Whoever remains out of it will have all the joys of this planet, and all the possibilities of growing in his potentiality to ultimate wisdom and to eternal life.

Those two trees have to be found! If God comes in between, throw him away. Adam and Eve were very poor, naked – only two! Now humanity is big enough. Rather than being driven by God, it can drive God out of paradise. He has lived in paradise long enough. Now just get lost!

Strange…you don't read me – the self-styled city of culture – you don't listen to me. Just my presence…?

I never go out, I never come into the ashram either, except these two hours in the evening. Living in my small room almost twenty-four hours a day, if my presence is corrupting your city, then it needs to be corrupted. Then it is not worth saving.

This ugly city will be destroyed by this egoist attitude, not by me; by these people who have been puffing the balloon of the ego that the city is cultural, religious. Go on puffing: soon the balloon will burst. It will be you, the editors and the political leaders, and the religious fanatics, who will destroy whatsoever culture you have. I don't know whether you have any or not.

As far as I'm concerned, culture has not happened yet in the world. And you are giving all proofs of being *un*cultured. Making a procession with my effigy on a donkey, you are showing your real faces.

Not a single newspaper, not a single citizen has condemned the procession, that it is polluting the culture and the religious heritage. No, this *is* your culture.

Bring as many donkeys as possible into your city, and they will purify your city. The day is not far away when only donkeys will be living in this city. Of course, donkeys don't corrupt anybody's culture; they are such silent, philosophical creatures.

I have always loved them from my very childhood. I have always wondered why these poor creatures are condemned. They look so silent, standing in the shadows of the walls or the trees. Just watch their faces: they look like Aristotle or Kant or Hegel or Feuerbach – great philosophers, thinking, thinking about great problems. Once in a while they give a shout – that is the shout that wakes other donkeys who are falling asleep.

Except that shout, they don't do any harm to anybody. They don't make processions, they don't shout ugly slogans. They are not worried at all that somebody will corrupt their culture.

If you have culture, nobody can corrupt it.

If you have religion, nobody can destroy it.

Because you don't have them – you have only fallacy, fantasy, imagination, belief, but no reality – that's why you are so afraid. Anybody can destroy your false belief systems. That is the fear, the paranoia.

But I am going to strike hard on all your false shadows, so you can be discovered in your true, authentic, original face.

The sutras:

Our Beloved Master,
Sanshō, a disciple of Rinzai, once said to Seppō, "The golden carp is out of the net! Tell me, what will it feed on?"

Zen always has many similar puzzles that cannot be solved. The ancientmost puzzle, out of which many such puzzles have arisen, is that one man was growing a goose in a bottle. When the goose was small, just out of the egg, he put it into the bottle. Then he went on feeding the goose in the bottle, until the whole bottle was full of the goose.

Now the goose is too big, it cannot be taken out from the mouth of the bottle. And the Zen masters have been asking: How to take the goose out without breaking the bottle, and without killing the goose? And people have been meditating on this: how to take the goose out without destroying the bottle, or destroying the goose. There seems to be no solution.

These riddles, these puzzles, are not for solutions; they bring a revolution when you get an insight. Hundreds of people have become enlightened through such small, absurd puzzles. Months and years they would meditate, and they would not find any way. There is no way…there is no question of finding any way. But because they were thinking only about the goose in the bottle for years, the whole mind dropped, all thinking stopped. Their only concern was how to bring the goose out from the bottle.

All logic failed, all reasoning failed, all thinking failed; the mind was of no help. They put the mind aside, and as they came to the space of no-mind, they laughed. They ran to the master, and seeing their smiling faces, the master would say, "So, the goose is out?" And the disciple would touch the feet of the master. He would say, "Yes, she has always been out. The bottle was an illusion."

You are always a buddha; your not being a buddha is an illusion. The bottle is an illusion, you are always out of the bottle. All prisons that surround you – of the mind, of the body, of money, of the world – are all irrelevant. As far as your innermost being is concerned, it is not touched by anything. It is always out. It just needs you to see the fact, and freedom comes from all directions to you.

Seppō said, "When you have got out of the net, I will tell you."

ONE SEED MAKES THE WHOLE EARTH GREEN

Seppō was a great master, just as Rinzai was a great master. Sanshō was only a disciple.

Seppō said to Sanshō, "When you have got out of the net, I will tell you. Right now, I don't see the point of wasting my time. You are not out, you will not understand. Just go and meditate. First get out of the net, and then I will answer you. In fact, then there is no need to answer."

This is the beauty of Zen. It brings your own consciousness to a point where there is no question, and no answer is needed. You have simply gone beyond questions and answers. You can sing a song, you can paint a beautiful painting, you can play music, you can dance, you can laugh, but you cannot say anything about what has happened to you.

Seppō said, "Just get out of the net, then come to me and I will tell you."

Sanshō said, "The renowned teacher of fifteen hundred monks cannot find even one word to say about this topic."

Seppō had a great monastery of fifteen hundred disciples. Sanshō taunts him, provokes him:

"The renowned teacher of fifteen hundred monks cannot find even one word to say about this topic?"

In fact, nobody can say a single word about the innermost freedom. Either you have it or you don't have it, but nobody can say anything about it. Even when you have it, you will not be able to say a single word. That, Sanshō does not understand yet.

Seppō said, "I am the chief abbot and have much to attend to.

"You just move away. First get out of the net and then

come. Right now, I don't have any time to waste with you."

It seems to be very unkind of Seppō, but it is not. He is helpless, as every buddha is helpless; there are things about which nothing can be said. You have to find them on your own accord.

If somebody says something, he is your enemy not a friend, because whatever he says will become a block in your search. You will start thinking you know the answer, what is the need of seeking? And the answer is borrowed, it is not yours.

If I drink water, my thirst is quenched.

If you drink the water, your thirst is quenched.

So are the eternal waters of life. Drink out of them. Nobody can give you an explanation – not even a single word – to indicate the direction.

Seppō was not unkind, he was simply telling him, "You are too childish, you don't understand what you are asking. You will have to find it yourself. First, get out of the net. Right now I have to attend to many affairs of my commune. I am the chief abbot."

On another occasion, some time later, Sanshō said to a monk, "Where have you just come from?"
The monk said, "Kwatz!"
Sanshō said, "Kwatz!"
The monk again said, "Kwatz!"
Sanshō could not understand. He said, "Kwatz? You are coming from Kwatz?"
The monk said, "If you strike me blindly, I shall say 'Kwatz!'"
It will be easy to understand if you just for a moment look

ONE SEED MAKES THE WHOLE EARTH GREEN

at the scientific theory of from where the universe has come. It was an explosion: Kwatz! – just a tremendous explosion, a chaos, and out of the chaos slowly things started solidifying.

The word 'kwatz' does not mean anything; it simply means an explosion of sound. That's what our 'Yaa-Hoo' means.

When you shout "Kwatz!" – watch where it hits you. It hits just under your navel. That's where you are coming from. The life center is just under your navel, two inches under the navel.

Hence in Japan – where they have found exactly the right center from where life has arisen in your body – when they want to commit suicide, they don't shoot themselves in the head, they don't shoot themselves in the heart, they stab underneath the navel, exactly two inches underneath. Just a good knife, and without any sound, without any torture, the man simply falls dead. Once the knife enters the center of your being, your life immediately leaves this body; this body is of no more use.

That is spoken of in Japan very respectfully, because unless a man knows through meditation where exactly the point is, he cannot commit suicide by hitting that point. Hitting that point is just like making a puncture in a tire. The air goes out. Hitting at the center of your being, the being simply flies out, searching for another womb if you are not yet enlightened. If you are enlightened, it disappears into the blue sky of the ultimate.

But "Kwatz!" is a beautiful sound. There are very few sounds which have no meaning, but immense significance.

When Sanshō said again, "Kwatz!"

The monk said, "If you strike me blindly, I shall say 'Kwatz!'"

I am always coming from Kwatz, if you are coming from Kwatz.

It looks very absurd to the outsiders, but not to the Zen people. Zen has a multidimensional environment of its own. It is very difficult to understand Japan if you don't understand Zen.

Here in the therapy groups there is a problem. So many Japanese are coming – and more will be on the way….

Sigmund Freud, and Carl Gustav Jung, and Alfred Adler, and Assagioli, and Fritz Perls – all the psychoanalysts of the West know only Christianity and Judaism. Christianity is just a branch of Judaism, nothing more. They don't understand anything about the East. All these therapies were developed in the West.

So every therapist tells his participants, "Deep down you must hate your father" – because Sigmund Freud's idea is that every girl is competitive with the mother, she hates the mother. She is jealous because the mother is monopolizing the father. She wants to have the father. So every girl hates the mother and loves the father, and vice versa: every boy loves the mother and hates the father. All these therapies basically are founded on father or mother fixation.

But therapists have been coming to me saying, "We are in a difficulty. If you tell a Japanese that he hates his mother, either he will kill himself or he will kill you." In Japan, to tell somebody that "You hate your mother," you have insulted his dignity. And when the dignity is insulted, humiliated, there are only two ways: either he kills you or he kills himself. But both cannot exist together anymore.

ONE SEED MAKES THE WHOLE EARTH GREEN

So the therapists have been asking me, "What to do? Our whole therapy is Jewish and Christian, and with the Japanese it does not apply at all." They have been brought up in a totally different atmosphere, where the mother is respected and loved, where the father is respected and loved. From the very childhood the father and mother persuade the child to go to the monastery to learn meditation, to go to a Zen monk to sit by his side just absorbing his fragrance, his presence, "because ultimately you have to reach to the flowering of buddhahood." It is a totally different orientation.

How can a boy hate his mother who has been telling him just to be himself? "Go to the monastery. Learn how to be self-centered" – and ultimately how to dissolve the center also, just to be nothing and pure, utterly empty. Only in emptiness no dust gathers; otherwise, everywhere dust gathers.

The father is persuading the child to learn from the masters, great masters. Even the emperors are sent by their fathers, "to learn something of your innermost being. If you don't know yourself, you are not worthy to be an emperor. First be an emperor of yourself."

How can you hate your father, who made you an emperor of yourself before giving you the succession of the outside empire? He has given you the inside empire.

Zen has certainly created a tremendous rebellion against all cultures, all civilizations.

As far as I can see, Zen is going to be paving the path for the new man to come, and for the new humanity to emerge. That's why I am talking so much on Zen. It is not without purpose. I want you to understand as deeply as possible.

Sanshō picked up his staff, and the monk put himself in readiness to receive a hit.

Can you find anywhere else in the world, somebody getting ready, bowing down, giving his head to be hit? Nowhere in the world. Either, if you are powerful, you will jump upon the person who is going to hit you; or if you are weak, you will escape in time before he hits you.

But this is absolutely Zen. The monk gets ready, on his knees, as if to pray, bowing down, giving his head – "Hit me." He has not said it, but his readiness says it: "If you hit me…even the hit from a master is a gift, a present which has no value in the marketplace, but which has value in the eternity of time."

Sanshō said, *"You go down a slope…."* When I hit you, you go down the slope of the mountain. There is no pleasure unless you run down it. And remember not to go slowly:

"There's no pleasure unless you run down" – with a tremendous urgency as if you are going somewhere.

"Then the cool breeze, and the beautiful sunrays, and your running down… Perhaps you may understand what you have not understood while you have been with me."

I am reminded of my own days of search.

I used to get up early, three o'clock in the morning, when it was absolutely dark and there were still three or four hours before the sunrise.

I was living by the side of a beautiful park, and there used to be nobody there. I used to run – it is a tremendous joy. You are again a deer in the park, again a lion in the forest. Something of tremendous spirit arises in you.

One old Sindhi used to have a small teashop – that was

ONE SEED MAKES THE WHOLE EARTH GREEN

the only shop, by the corner of the garden – for people coming in the daytime to the garden. That was the only garden, with very beautiful and ancient trees. He had a good business selling tea. He used to sleep in a small shelter in the night.

When I used to run, many times he said, "Forgive me, sir. You wake me up. I know it's you, but I come out of my sleep perspiring and trembling, because at this time nobody comes here, and sometimes you are too much" – because sometimes I used to run backwards.

There was a huge field full of bamboos. They made such a great shadow that in the fullmoon night the road was covered with the shadows of the bamboos. So when I used to enter the shadows, nobody could see me, and when I would come out of the shadows suddenly, that old Sindhi would jump up from his cot.

He would say, "Again? How many times I have convinced myself that this is that same young man, utterly crazy! But you will kill me one day, my heart beats so hard. Suddenly out of the shadows somebody comes, and that too, running backwards...!" In India, the mythology is that ghosts run backwards, that was the trouble. "How to make the distinction that you are really you, not a ghost?"

One day it happened – it was three o'clock – a milkman must have awoken early. He used to come nearer five or six, but perhaps he was not having a good sleep, perhaps there were too many mosquitoes, something may have been... He arrived early, and he had two buckets full of milk.

When I came out of the shadows, dancing backwards, he threw away both the buckets and ran. And I, thinking that he had misunderstood me, ran after him! The more I ran, the faster he ran. I said, "It is strange…."

The old Sindhi was watching the whole scene. He said, "You will kill him! Why are you following him?"

I said, "I simply want to tell him that I am not a ghost."

The old Sindhi said, "Nobody will believe it. Ghosts always say that! You just give me those two buckets. In the morning that fellow will come, and I will give him the buckets and explain the situation."

For years I inquired of the old Sindhi whether the man had come. He said, "No, those two buckets are still there."

I said, "Have you got any idea where he has gone?"

He said, "No idea. Oftentimes I think you have killed him. He could not have survived that strange experience of a ghost following him."

But I made every effort to find the man. Finally I found him; he lived in a nearby village. So I went there with those two buckets.

The moment he saw me, he started, jumping. He said, "No! Don't come here!"

I said, "I have come just to give back your buckets."

He said, "I don't want anything!" – with closed eyes, so he wouldn't see me.

I said, "At least see me, just look at my feet. They are not the way ghosts' feet are, backwards!"

The man looked at my feet. He said, "So you are not a ghost?"

I said, "One day I will become one, but right now I am not."

He said, "My God! I have been going around almost two miles unnecessarily just to avoid that spot where you came running backwards! Don't do that. Anybody…"

I said, "You don't know the beauty of it."

He said, "Beauty?"

I said, "You don't know the blessing of it."

He said, "Don't persuade me."

I said, "Just once, you come along with me."

He thought for a moment, and he said, "It is better I should come so that the fear of that place is gone."

So the next day I picked him up from this village in my car, and brought him to my house, and we both went jogging backwards.

The old Sindhi jumped out of his cot. He said, "My God! Where have you found this other ghost?"

I said, "He is not a ghost."

He said, "I have told you, all ghosts say that!"

I said, "This is the same man who has dropped his milk buckets."

He said, "Where did you find him? You dug him up from the grave?"

I said, "You bring your torch and look at his feet. He is a live man, he has not died. And look at the buckets: you know the buckets, they have been lying with you for years."

He said, "It is better I should change from this place; it is becoming too heavy. Tomorrow you may bring a third one – and in the darkness it is very difficult to distinguish. Can't you stop this jogging backwards?"

I said, "It is so beautiful…it is such an ecstasy."

He said, "What?"

I said, "Unless you taste it…" I said, "Ask the milkman."

The milkman said, "It is true, it makes you feel so free."

The old man said, "Then I will try tomorrow."

His wife said, "No! You are not going to join these people. They are crazy, and they are persuading you."

I said, "Let him have a taste. Don't be worried, nothing will happen. I take the responsibility. And one day you will join us."

She said, "You think I will join you? Then it is better we both join together. If something happens, it happens to both of us. I don't want to live alone without my husband." So they both joined.

I used to live with a friend, a very rich man. He had given me half of his bungalow. When he saw four people – three men and one woman – he freaked out!

He said, "It was okay when you were doing it alone. I know you. But I don't know these people – whether they are men, women, or just ghosts. And where have you found this woman? Either you drop this or you take possession of the whole bungalow. I have another bungalow, I will leave."

I said, "That will be just great, because then I can entertain new ghosts, even allow them to sleep here just to get them up in time – three o'clock."

Actually he moved.

Sanshō is saying rightly,
"When you go down a slope, there is no pleasure unless you run down it" at which he struck the monk.
The monk said, "You robber!" and went off,
running on the slope.

Zen creates beautiful anecdotes.

What he is trying to say, I am telling you every day.

Go in – not slowly, but with your total consciousness,

with an urgency as if this is the last moment, just like a spear, piercing more than running, because the slope is very small. From your head to your being, there is very little distance. Unless you go really fast, breaking all the bridges, breaking all the obstacles, you will not reach to your ultimate being.

That's what Sanshō meant, and the monk understood when he said, *"You robber!"* It is a very loving expression. He is saying, "You have robbed me completely. You have convinced me completely. My heart is your heart, my being is in your hands."

Another monk present at the scene asked, "The monk just now – how can he enter?"

He understood – he was a follower of Sanshō – he understood what Sanshō meant by running and not going slowly.

The monk asked, *"How can he enter* by running down the slope?"

Sanshō commented, "That chap had been to see the former teacher".

"He has gone running to see his old master. The old master could not convince him; I have managed to convince him. The old master was saying the same thing to him, but he missed. Now he has gone back to the old master saying, 'You were right. It was just my thickness of intelligence, my hard skin, that nothing penetrated. But Sanshō did the job within a minute. He gave me such a hit on the head, and I ran down the whole slope of the mountain.'"

He was right. These are symbolic words.

Sanshō is saying, "I am hitting you, and from that point there is a slope from the head to the heart to the being.

Go running, don't stop anywhere, and don't be slow. Nobody knows about the next second; this second may be the last one." So he has gone to pay his respects to his old master.

Buson wrote:

> *The sea at springtime.*
> *All day it rises and falls,*
> *yes, rises and falls.*

You have to visualize again:
The sea at springtime. All day it rises and falls, yes, rises and falls.
He is saying, without saying it, the ultimate truth of your being: "You rise but you don't rise to the ultimate peak from where there is no fall. You rise a little bit and fall again. Again you hear another master, you rise a little more and you fall again.

"Unless you rise to the ultimate peak, to the hilltop from where there is no coming back, you have been doing just a futile exercise like the ocean waves: rising and falling, rising and falling, since eternity. When will you stop this? When will you rise and rise and rise to where there is no fall again?"

This I call buddhahood.
This I call the awakened being.

Maneesha has asked a question:

Our Beloved Master,
Do we really have to come back from the let-go? Last

night, especially, it felt as if You could have talked us into enlightenment!

Maneesha, I have Nivedano ready. The moment I see you are going beyond the limit from where you will not be able to return, I immediately call Nivedano.

You have to be here with me. So much has to be done for humanity. So I take you to the point, but not to the ultimate point. I just allow you a glimpse, and the moment I see you are going ahead, I immediately call you back.

You have to be here while I am here. So much remains undone. The whole of humanity, without knowing it, is waiting for someone to make them conscious, alert, to help them to become buddhas. They may not know, they may even fight you.

It used to happen... The most important German philosopher, Immanuel Kant, never married – not that he was in favor of celibacy, but because he was a great thinker.

A woman had asked him; he said, "I will have to think about it, it is a great matter."

He took three years of deep research about all the points in favor of marriage and against marriage. They were equal.

His servant said, "Don't waste time. Although you have found the pros and cons equal, one thing more remains in favor of marriage."

He said, "What is that?"

The servant said, "The experience. Without marriage you will not have any experience. With marriage you will have some experience – I don't say good or bad – but some experience certainly. That remains one point more in favor."

It was so convincing that he went immediately to the house of the woman and knocked on the door. The father opened it, and Kant said, "I am willing to marry your daughter."

He said, "My son, you are too late. She is married, she has two children. What have you been doing all this time?"

He said, "I have been researching all the points pro and con."

The old man said, "You found more points favorable?"

He said, "No, it was my servant who said to me that it is always better to have the experience than not to have it. One never knows, something good may come out of it. And even if it turns out something bad, it makes you more experienced."

So he remained a bachelor. No other woman ever asked him, and he was not a man to ask anybody.

He was dependent on this servant. The servant went on asking for more salary, and he had to give it, because no other servant was able to stay with him. He was a very strange fellow, and the most strange thing was that he used to work like a clock.

When he used to go to the university, people would fix their watches. It was enough that he was going; that meant their watches were not right. When he would come back, every day at the same time... Even on Sundays when there was no need to go to the university, just to keep the routine he would go to the university, sit in the library and come back at the same time as usual.

At three o'clock in the morning he had to be awakened, and at nine o'clock in the evening he had to be forced into bed. That all had to be done by the servant. He was paying him an immense salary, with the condition that when it was nine, "Whatever happens – I may fight with you, that I have some immediately urgent work to do – don't listen to me. You have to force me into bed. Even if you have to beat me, you are allowed. But remember, I will give you a good fight!"

It was a strange scene. Every evening at nine o'clock, every morning at three o'clock – it was such a chaos that the whole neighborhood woke up. The servant would be pulling him out, and he would be going back under the blanket. He would be shouting, abusing him, and the servant would be beating him, slapping him.

This is the situation of the whole of humanity.

Maneesha, you all have to live to wake up people even against their will, in spite of them. Don't bother if they hit you, if they cry, if they shout; you go on pulling them. They have to be made buddhas!

That's why I don't allow you to go beyond the limit. I am watching everyone closely.

It is time for Sardar Gurudayal Singh.

Hiram T. Horace III, the American diplomat in Paris, is approached by his son, Hiram Junior.

"Dad," asks Hiram Junior, "what does inflation mean?"

"Well, son," says Hiram Senior, "it means a general price increase."

"Really?" asks Hiram Junior. "And what difference does that make?"

"Well, son," explains Hiram T. Horace III, "I would

put it this way: here in Paris, before inflation, for me life was wine, restaurants and women. Since inflation, now it is beer, eating at home and your mother!"

Ziggy Zoldoz, a Czechoslovakian citizen, is condemned to a jail sentence of fifteen years for calling the Communist Party chairman an idiot.

Bernie Beanball, the foreign correspondent for the *New Age Times*, asks a government official why Ziggy's sentence is so severe. "Surely," says Bernie, "the jail sentence for personal insults is never more than twelve months?"

"That's right," snaps the party man, "but he was not condemned for insults. He was convicted for revealing a state secret!"

Farmer Scrumpy decides to pay a call on his old friend, Farmer Zeke. He finds Zeke leaning on the fence of the hog pen, smoking his pipe and humming a song.

"Hi, Zeke," says Scrumpy, looking around the farm. "How have things been with you lately?"

"Ah, pretty tolerable," replies Zeke. "I had some trees that needed cutting down, but a tornado came along and saved me the trouble."

"Really?" asks Scrumpy.

"Yup," says Zeke. "Then the branches were lying there and needed burning, but lightning set fire to them and saved me the trouble."

"Really?" asks Scrumpy. "So what are you going to do now?"

"Well, nothing much," replies Zeke, sucking on his pipe. "I figured I would just wait here until the potatoes get shaken out of the ground by an earthquake!"

ONE SEED MAKES THE WHOLE EARTH GREEN

Nivedano...

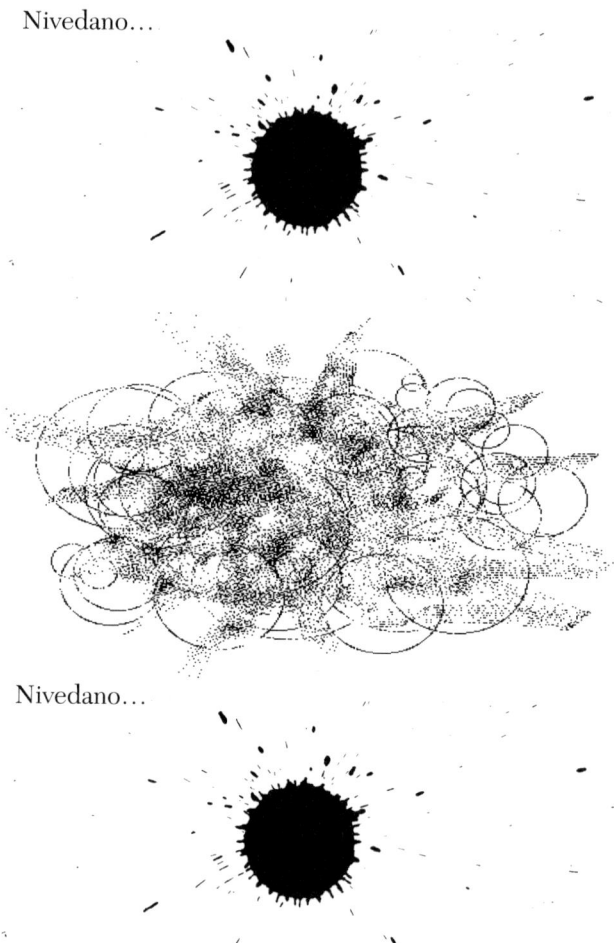

Nivedano...

Be silent...Close your eyes, and feel your body to be completely frozen.

This is the right moment to look inwards. But go running, with your full consciousness, your total life energy, and an urgency that – one never knows – this may be the last moment of your life.

You have to become a buddha. Go just piercing your astral body to the very center of your being.

As you go closer, as you go deeper, a great silence descends on you. A little more…and a peace that you have never known before surrounds you. A little more… and you are at the center of your being. This moment you are the most fortunate beings on the earth.

A great ecstasy starts flowering in the very center of your being, like a lotus. The fragrance is of another world.

The only quality you have to remember is: Witness everything, but don't get identified with anything.

You are not the body, you are not the mind, you are not the astral body full of light. You are only a witness, centered, just watching, reflecting like a mirror. On this mirror no dust ever gathers.

To make it clear, Nivedano…

Relax, but remember to witness.
Just be a witness of everything that is happening.
The moment you are only a witness, you will feel

you are melting into an ocean, just like ice melts.

Gautama the Buddha Auditorium at this moment has become an ocean of consciousness without any ripples. You have merged into each other. This is the first experience, the first glimpse.

This seed will grow in time, and suddenly one day you will find the spring has come! You are a buddha, the awakened one – the ultimate search of all seekers of truth.

Collect as much ecstasy, as much blissfulness, as much benediction…and persuade the buddha to come with you to the circumference of your life. In your everyday work, in your words, in your gestures, in your silences, he has to be present.

Slowly slowly you disappear, and only buddha remains. From that point, when only the buddha remains, you can jump into the cosmos, a quantum leap, and disappear without leaving any trace behind.

This is the ultimate goal of existence for all living beings – particularly for human beings, because they are the highest evolved.

Before Nivedano calls you back, persuade the buddha. It is not someone else, it is your very being.

Nivedano…

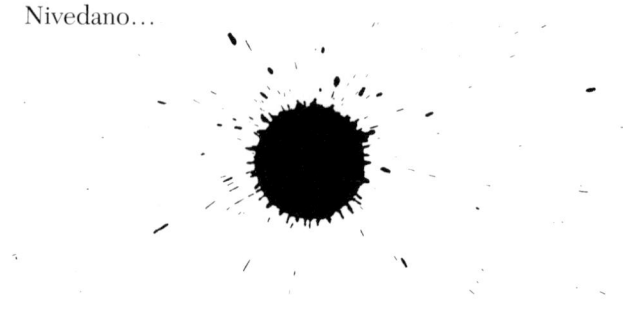

Come back...

But now come back as the buddha, filled with joy, blissfulness, grace, a deep silence.

Sit for a few moments just to remember the path, the golden path that you have traveled. And just rejoice in the fact that you have been able to melt and merge, that you have been able to encounter your authentic self, the buddha.

And remember to share your fire, to share your gold with all and sundry, friend and enemy, the acquaintance and the stranger. The whole humanity is ours – they may not know, but *we* know. They may struggle against us, but we can only feel compassion for them.

Remember, one seed can make the whole earth green.

Okay, Maneesha?
Yes, Beloved Master.

1,758,640,175 Devils

January 15, 1989

ONE SEED MAKES THE WHOLE EARTH GREEN

OUR BELOVED MASTER,
*Once, a monk asked Fuketsu,
"What is the buddha?"
Fuketsu replied, "The bamboo whips
of Mount Jorin."
Another monk then asked, "What is the buddha?"
Fuketsu answered, "What is not the buddha?"
A third monk said to Fuketsu, "The Western
Patriarch came bringing his message;
I ask you to tell me it point-blank!"
At this, Fuketsu replied, "When one dog
barks at nothing, a thousand monkeys
really show their teeth."
On another occasion a monk asked, "What is the
meaning of Daruma's coming from the West?"
Fuketsu said, "We know all the windings of the
mountain stream, but not the mountain itself."*

Friends, today I am going to talk first about religion and the crime that it has committed against humanity, nature, environment, ecology.

Religion's crimes are many, innumerable, but the worst crime is that it has placed man at the center of existence. It has given the idea to the whole of humanity that the whole existence is for your use: you are God's greatest creation.

A man-oriented vision of existence is bound to create catastrophes in nature, it is bound to destroy the ecological balance, it is bound to give man the strange idea of an ego.

The Bible says God created man in his own image, and man has believed it. Just look at your face in the mirror: is it God's face in the mirror?

The truth is that Christianity has been befooling humanity. It is not that God made man in his own image, it is man who has made God in *his* own image. And all the scriptures of all the religions have given man a strange licentiousness over nature, over animals and birds. That has culminated in destroying many species of animals, birds. It has destroyed millions of trees for no reason. Every second that passes, one football ground is cleaned of all greenery, all trees.

When India became independent, it had thirty-three million hectares of trees. Today it has only eleven million hectares.

This man-centered view begins with Genesis, in the Bible. In Genesis it says:

"Be fruitful and multiply, and replenish the earth and subdue it; and have dominion over the fish of the sea and over the fowl of the air and over every living thing that moveth upon the earth."

This is the ultimate crime that has made man violent against nature, given him the freedom to conquer innocent animals, to destroy them. It has made man barbarious.

Now we are suffering because all those trees have been destroyed and more are being destroyed continuously. There is a certain balance in existence. These trees are your brothers and your sisters, there is no question of dominion. You exhale carbon dioxide, they inhale it. They exhale oxygen, you inhale it. Such a deep relationship... You cannot exist without trees, nor can trees exist without you; your existence is so deeply rooted in each other.

As trees have become less and less, the level of oxygen in the air has gone down and down and down. Now you are living only a fragmentary life. You may not have thought about it....

Why don't you breathe fully? Your lungs have six

thousand sacs which have to be filled, but you breathe shallowly, so only two thousand sacs are filled, and four thousand remain stagnant, filled with dead carbon dioxide which is the cause of millions of diseases. It reduces your lifespan, it weakens your spirit, it destroys your intelligence. You are living at the minimum just because of this statement in Genesis that you "have dominion over the fish of the sea and over the fowl of the air and over every living thing that moveth upon the earth."

Man has killed so many beautiful species of animals just for his food, has killed so many birds – whole species have disappeared.

In India, the lion was the national animal, but stupid hunters – particularly the British hunters, who have been in power in this country for almost three hundred years – destroyed all the lions, the most beautiful animal in existence. Such a dignity, such power, such grandeur! And what were they doing? – just decorating their sitting-rooms with the stuffed heads of the lions.

Today the whole species is on the verge of disappearing. There are not more than two dozen lions in the whole of India. The Indian government had to change its national animal from the lion to the tiger, because lions are going to disappear. When a lion dies, it is never replaced.

And it is not only the British Christians who destroyed them; even Hindu monks sit on a lion's skin. You will not believe how stupid people can be.

Religion seems to give a certain stupidity to people who were born intelligent.

The Hindu monks sit on the skin of a lion – and of course, one lion has to be killed for one monk – and the ideology that they preach is that by sitting on the lion's skin you can remain celibate. My foot! Stupidity has no limit.

What does the lion's skin have to do with your celibacy? Lions are not celibate; one has never heard about a lion who was celibate. What scientific proof is there? I don't know a single monk who is a celibate, and I have known thousands of monks – Hindus, Jainas....

Just now two books have come out about one of the richest sects of the Jainas, Terapanth. The sect is headed by Acharya Tulsi. Seventeen hundred monks are under him, and three times more nuns – and all are sexually perverted.

These two books that have just come out, Acharya Tulsi tried hard to get the government to ban them. But the publisher of the books is also a follower of the same sect. He knows that what is written in those two books by ex-monks of Acharya Tulsi is absolutely true. He said, "I will fight against the government and go to the Supreme Court. They cannot prevent a truth!"

Once I was in Acharya Tulsi's camp for seven days. I could not believe...so many monks, so many nuns came in contact with me, and they told me that such perversion is going on behind the scenes – and even Acharya Tulsi is not an exception. Homosexuality is widely prevalent, heterosexuality is widely prevalent. Those nuns are used almost like prostitutes. They go on preaching about celibacy, and their own reality is all kinds of perversions.

One of the ex-members of the cult had come to me directly when he left the cult. He wanted to write the book, but I said, "Wait a little. Nobody will listen to you.

You just create some status for yourself and then write the book. The book is absolutely essential" – because he himself was the victim of Acharya Tulsi's sexuality, not to say of other monks.

Beautiful Jaina girls are invited to become nuns. It is thought, it is preached, it has been propagated for hundreds of years that to become a nun is to become holy: you bring prestige and blessings to your family too. So when they see a beautiful girl, they invite the family: "The girl has such spiritual powers that she needs to be initiated as a nun." The family is happy, the community is happy, the girl is happy that she has been chosen as a spiritual being of tremendous possibilities. But the reality is totally different. She has been chosen because she is beautiful, young, and the monks are sitting there hungry.

I made this statement, and not a *single* Indian newspaper had the courage to print it! And when my press office asked, inquired what had happened to my statement – I take the whole responsibility for it, you need not be worried! – they said, "We are feeling very nervous to print it." And it has not been printed.

Perhaps they have been bribed by the followers of Acharya Tulsi. Perhaps the government is behind it, because Acharya Tulsi has a hold over many votes and much money that he manages through his followers to donate to the political parties who are in power.

All religions are sexually perverted. They have to be. Their only creative and positive act through the centuries is AIDS-positive.

And because Genesis says, "Be fruitful" – that means populate the earth more and more – "and multiply" – not even double, but multiply – that's why the Christian pope and the bishops and the cardinals and the priests are all against birth control: because it goes against Genesis, the very foundation of their religion.

So this whole population explosion, which is going to kill half of humanity through utter starvation, who is responsible for it? Genesis – and these stupid bishops and popes, and cardinals and priests.

You will be surprised to know that when Ronald Reagan came to power, he immediately cut the budget for controlling the poor countries' population, because he was a fundamentalist, fascist Christian. Since he has been in power, he has fulfilled the statement of Genesis: "Be fruitful and multiply."

When India became independent, it had only four hundred million people. Now it has nine hundred million people, and by the end of this century it will be one billion human beings. After forty years it will double: there will be two billion people in India. From where are you going to get food?

Right now, half the country is starving, and more than half the country is undernourished. Even a politician, the chief minister of Haryana, has come with the statement – because his state is starving – that if this situation continues, India will become a subhuman species. It will lose all intelligence, it will lose all strength and power, it will lose all the dignity of human beings.

It is very rare to hear the truth from a politician, very rare to hear the truth from a religious man.

In his book, *In God's Name,* David Yallop exposes the corruption of the Vatican. He tells how Pope John Paul –

the pope before this Polack pope – had ordered an investigation of the Vatican Bank after reports that it was involved in money laundering.

The pope had also made it clear that under his direction the church would approve of birth control.

Suddenly, after these two radical moves, thirty-three days after being made pope, this healthy man died of a heart attack. His personal notes, will, and medicine bottles mysteriously disappeared. Before the cause of death could be confirmed, his body was embalmed, a process which makes it impossible to detect the presence of poison. Many people feel he was murdered.

The new pope, a Polack, promoted the head of the same bank to archbishop. For this man who had been the head of the bank, the government of Italy has issued an arrest warrant – but they cannot enter the Vatican. The Vatican is a country of eight square miles just in the middle of Rome, the capital of Italy. The sovereign head of the religion and the country is the pope. Of course, nobody can enter there to arrest him. And they know perfectly well that he has to be arrested by the Italian government if he goes out of the Vatican, because of what they have been doing through the bank...

It is the greatest mafia. All the heroin money – not a small account, six hundred million dollars per year! – they are turning into white money. This is the whole function of the Vatican Bank. John Paul was a man of great intelligence. He wanted to find out the facts about the bank, because it is committing the greatest crime, for which millions of young people are suffering in jails.

After only thirty-three days... This is the least time any pope has been a pope. He was perfectly healthy; he had no record of any heart diseases, and he was found sitting in his bed, dead, clutching a paper in his hand, in which he had written his will and made two points clear: that the bank should be completely investigated, and if there is any crime being committed, the persons should be punished. And second, the situation has changed completely since the days of Genesis. Birth control should be allowed, and all kinds of birth control methods, pills, should be allowed to humanity – particularly to Catholics. It is not the time to multiply.

This paper that he was clutching in his hand – and he was dead – this paper also disappeared. And they did not get a certificate from a medical expert that he had died naturally; they immediately embalmed the body without telling anyone. After embalming the body there is no way to find whether the person has been poisoned or not.

As far as I can see, he was certainly murdered because he was going against the criminal bank, and against the criminal attitude of the Christians – they go on being against abortion, against birth control pills, against any kind of method that can prevent the population explosion.

This is not a unique case.

Who crucified Jesus? The religious rabbis, the high priest, the head rabbi of the great temple of the Jews in Jerusalem. They *all*, without any exception, wanted this innocent young man, who was only thirty-three years old, to be crucified, for no reason at all. He had not committed any crime. He had not murdered anyone, he had not raped anyone.

Even the Roman governor of Judea was surprised to know that they wanted to crucify Jesus. And the Roman governor present in Jerusalem, Pontius Pilate, wanted to free him, because he could not see any harm. "Perhaps he says things which Jews don't want to hear, so close your ears and go on your way. Don't listen! But this is not a cultured and human way. Because you disagree with him and you cannot even give arguments to this uneducated Jesus, crucifixion is the answer...? But Pontius Pilate hoped that at the last moment...

Every year when the Jewish holidays start, the criminals who have been condemned are crucified. Three persons, three criminals were going to be crucified, and one was Jesus, who was not a criminal at all. Pontius Pilate was hoping that the high priest of the temple – the highest post for the rabbis, the learned scholars of Judaism, who had the right to release one person from crucifixion – would ask for Jesus to be released, because he had not committed any crime. But even the high priest, with all the thousands of rabbis surrounding the temple, shouted that Barabbas, a criminal beyond conception...

Barabbas had murdered seven people, he had raped many women; he was a perfect drunkard. He had remained in jail almost his whole life. Every time he was released, within two days he would be back – he had murdered somebody or he had raped some woman. Now finally they decided he should be crucified – he was incurable. It was a shock to Pontius Pilate, but all the rabbis, including the chief rabbi, shouted, "We want Barabbas to be released."

Even Barabbas could not believe it. He knew Jesus. Once in a while he had heard him, and he had loved the young man. He was saying beautiful things. He had hoped that if he could remain out of jail, he could listen more to this young man.

ONE SEED MAKES THE WHOLE EARTH GREEN

Jesus had been talking to people for only three years, and not to many people, because everybody was afraid of the religious hierarchy: if you are found in company with Jesus you may be punished also. So only a few young people, who had the courage and the guts, followed him and listened to him.

Barabbas, whenever he had the chance to be out of jail, went to hear him. And when he saw that he was to be released, and this poor fellow with great ideas, with beautiful visions, is being crucified, even Barabbas said to the people, "It is absolutely criminal. It is perfectly right for me to be crucified, I have done enough crimes! But this young man...he has not even started living, he is only thirty-three."

And within seven days Barabbas killed another man. But it was the rule of the Roman empire that once a man is released from crucifixion by the mercy of the emperor, he cannot be condemned to death again. It is a tremendously dramatic story – far more dramatic than the story of Jesus.

Christians say Jesus did many miracles, but no contemporary Jewish record exists. If those miracles really had happened – a dead man had been resurrected, water had been turned into wine, with one loaf of bread he fed thousands of people, he walked on water – do you think a man like this would go unnoticed by the contemporaries? Not a single reference even to the name of Jesus is made by any contemporary literature.

But Barabbas really was a man of miracles. This was a miracle. After committing seven murders, many rapes, he is released...and it is asked that he be released by the most holy and religious rabbis, *unanimously!* Is it not a miracle?

And after seven days – it was just his habit – he killed a man, he raped some woman, he was arrested again. But now he could not be crucified, so he was sent to Greece. That was the way. If somebody cannot be crucified, once he has been released out of the mercy of the emperor, he was sent to the coal mines in Greece. Those coal mines had become so deep, and the technology was almost nil, that almost every month thousands of people died, because the mine would collapse.

Just when Barabbas entered the coal mine, the third day the mine collapsed. Everybody down the mine – and there were almost two thousand people – everybody died except Barabbas. Don't you call it a miracle?

Even the emperor, the Roman emperor, was impressed. His queen too was much impressed – "This is the real man of God!" – so he was called to Rome, the capital. The games were going to begin, and in the games one special event was fighting with a lion who had been kept hungry for many days.

The emperor wanted to know whether this Barabbas was really a man of God, so Barabbas was put into the stadium. A hungry lion was released, and Barabbas fought with his totality, because there was no need to save anything; the lion was going to kill him.

But you will be surprised: he killed the lion. With such totality and such urgency, when life is at stake, who cares for anything? Even the lion became afraid – and he killed it with his bare hands!

Even the emperor could not believe his eyes. It had never happened before! And the queen wanted at least to touch the robe of Barabbas, so she stood outside the stadium gate, and when Barabbas was taken out, she just touched his robe, and she said, "You are a man of God."

But all these years he could not forget the face of Jesus. That innocent face, that young face, that peaceful and silent face had been haunting him day and night. So as he was released – the emperor had to release him – he immediately found an underground group of people who had turned to Christianity. He joined the group, and the day he joined the group and accepted a cross to hang around his neck, he was caught immediately and crucified. No miracle happened. He died as a Christian.

Why was Jesus crucified?

Religion cannot tolerate any man with new visions, with new dreams, with new hopes for mankind, with new promises to be fulfilled. No religion can tolerate the emergence of anybody who has a new image of man. They feel hurt. That means their scriptures have been wrong, that up to now what they have been worshipping has been stupid. For this single man they cannot leave their whole heritage.

They have no argument against Jesus, or against Socrates, or against al-Hillaj Mansoor; their only argument is crucifixion. Religion has committed so many crimes for centuries. Every religion thinks others are wrong, and to put them right, the simple way is to cut off their heads. Christians have been killing Jews, Mohammedans; Mohammedans have been killing Christians, Hindus; Hindus have been killing Mohammedans, Buddhists – in the name of God! What kind of God have you got?

According to a book by Corrado Balducci, a diplomat

of the Vatican, the devil's army consists of exactly one billion, seven hundred and fifty-eight million, six hundred and forty thousand, one hundred and seventy-five devils. Certainly this Vatican diplomat must have visited hell!

And how many people are in the army of God, may I ask? Just those three fellows – God, the Holy Ghost, and the only begotten son, Jesus? Is there any possibility of God winning against the devil?

I will repeat the number so you can remember it. The devil's army consists of exactly one billion, seven hundred and fifty-eight million, six hundred and forty thousand, one hundred and seventy-five devils. There is no hope for humanity.

Perhaps that's why God has escaped to some faraway star, with his only begotten son and the Holy Ghost – seeing the situation.

One wonders how these people come to these conclusions. This diplomat, if he has been to hell... In Christianity you cannot return from hell. Once you are in hell you are forever in hell, for eternity. How did he manage, against his own religion, to come out of hell? And without going to hell, do you think anybody can count this big a number, just sitting in the Vatican?

And no Christian has even questioned the stupidity of this man. That surprises me. I simply cannot believe it. On the one hand, Christianity says, if you fall into hell, it is finished; the door is closed forever, and eternally you will burn in hellfire.

It was on this point that one of the most significant thinkers of this century, Bertrand Russell, dropped out of Christianity – on this point particularly. He wrote a book, *Why I Am Not a Christian,* and the first point is that "I cannot conceive that in one life…" because Christianity believes only in one life. In Hinduism, in Jainism, in Buddhism, you can commit millions of sins because millions of lives are available, backwards and forwards. You can go on doing so many sins, there is no need to count. But in Christianity, in Judaism, in Mohammedanism, there is only one life.

"In one life," Bertrand Russell asks the question, "how many sins can I commit? All the sins that I have committed, and all the sins that I wanted to commit but I have not committed, and all the sins I have dreamt of committing… Even if all these are considered to be sins, the hardest judge in the world cannot put me in jail for more than four and a half years. An eternity of hellfire? – I have not committed enough sins yet!"

This is so absurd, that a man like Bertrand Russell… He has many other points, but this is the basic point: that it is absolutely absurd. If you go on committing sins from the time you are born, day and night, till you enter your grave, then too an eternity of hellfire is not justified. Seventy years continuous sinning – without sleeping, without eating – then too, seventy years are only seventy years. Even that many sins…although you cannot commit that many sins. You will need some time to eat, some time to sleep, some time to love, some time to go to the movies. And what will happen to television?

But Christianity goes on, without giving any reasoning, insisting that if you commit sins… How many sins? At least a number should be given, that if you commit one dozen sins nothing is said about it. You can commit one sin, you can commit a thousand sins…the punishment is the same. What kind of justice is this?

And these people who have been counting the devils…

In the Middle Ages they were killing women, calling them witches.

The word 'witch' is not a bad word. In its origins it means a wise woman. But Christianity polluted the word, destroyed its beauty. And what was the process – how do you find a witch, how do you prove that she is a witch? Once proved, the only punishment was to burn her alive at the crossroads in the main part of the city.

A special court was arranged by the pope to find all the witches and destroy them, because they were "possessed by the devil."

Nobody knows anything about God, nobody knows anything about the devil, and thousands and thousands of women were burnt alive! How did they manage it? – a simple process.

Anybody could inform, even anonymously: "I suspect a certain woman in my neighborhood is a witch." That woman would be caught immediately by the court, forced into jail, tortured, beaten, sexually abused.

I remembered those women when my back was bad, some eight years ago. A traction machine was brought to pull my body – the legs in one direction, the head in another direction – to put the backbone straight. At that time I remembered that this traction machine was invented by the Christians to torture women. I have known a little bit of torture on that machine, but those women were torn apart. Sometimes legs would come off…sometimes there was no need to burn them alive. The head would come off….

Big blocks of ice would be put on their chests. Unless they confessed, there was no way of getting out of the jail:

"Confess that you are having sexual relations with the devil!" Naturally, anybody would think it is better to confess than to go through all this torture. And this torture would continue until they confessed; there was no way out.

And the bishops who were torturing them would teach them how they have to confess in the court. When they confessed that, "Yes, I have been having a sexual relationship with the devil," then the priest would tell them, "You have to tell the court how you recognize the devil. You have to tell them that he has a forked penis" – so he can enter into the women from both the holes – "that's how I recognized that it is a devil."

Those poor women had to confess this in the court. And the court would ask, "How do you recognize it is the devil, not a man?" Then they would describe the genital mechanism of the devil. It has certainly to be special, forked; that was enough proof.

They created the confession, they created the proof, and the woman was burnt alive. They destroyed thousands of women in the name of God – because the devil *has* to be destroyed.

But now, seeing the number of devils…I don't think that just by killing a few thousand women by burning you can destroy the devil. You are destroying women, the devil will find other women – and so many devils!

Strange…you should have burnt the devil, not the woman. The woman was a victim; the criminal was the devil. But it is a strange logic: the victim is burned because you cannot find the devil anywhere.

No devil exists, nor does any God exist. These are fictions created by the religions to torture humanity, to exploit humanity, to create fear and greed in mankind.

And the theology of Christians has not changed. It is still the same.

Moses, the founder of Judaism, certainly lied to the Jews when he said, "I have been told by God that you are the chosen people of the world, and he has told me to lead you to the holy land, Israel."

If he had been told exactly the address where Israel was, then why did it take forty years to find Israel? Forty long years of wandering in the deserts of Saudi Arabia... And my feeling, without any doubt, is that what he called Israel was simply to hide the fact that he had lied. Israel is just a poor place, mountainous, not rich; in no way can it be called God's holy place.

Moses recognized it when he left the people he had brought from Egypt. Almost three fourths of them had died of hunger, of thirst...forty years of wandering in the desert. The third generation of the people had come into being, who did not care much about Moses; they didn't know anything about who this fellow was. Seeing the situation, he simply told them, "This is the place."

But life was going to be very hard, harder than it was in Egypt. And for four thousand years the Jews have suffered more than they ever suffered in Egypt. In Egypt they were slaves, but even that slavery was far better than this false promise and hope. And, seeing the situation, he must have been thinking, "These young people don't know me, their fathers or forefathers had come with me. Seeing this hard land, unproductive, they are not going to forgive me for leading them to this place." Just as an excuse to escape from Israel, he said, "One of our tribes has got lost in the desert. I am going to find them while you manage the holy land of God."

Moses went in search of the lost tribe, which had come to Kashmir. They had settled in Kashmir. Kashmir looks like a holy place. The first Moghul emperor, Babar – when he came to conquer India, he had to enter through Kashmir – looking at the beauty of Kashmir, he said, "If there is any paradise, it is here. It is here!"

Moses came to Kashmir; his grave is in Kashmir. And because he had given a false idea of superiority, the Jews have suffered immensely. Their suffering has not yet come to an end. The whole responsibility goes to Moses.

Religious founders have been lying in every possible way. Moses lied to his people that on the Sinai mountain he had seen God, and God had given him ten commandments. Nobody has seen God.

Just think of yourself: if by chance you come across God, what are you going to do? Hit him hard and kill him, because all the suffering that humanity has been going through for centuries and centuries is the responsibility of the God who created man, who created the world.

What was the need? Existence was perfectly silent and beautiful. What was the need to create Genghis Khan, and Tamerlane, and Nadirshah? Just between these three, they killed one hundred million people.

What was the need to create Adolf Hitler? And strangely enough, he killed God's chosen people: six million Jews in Germany! And he himself proclaimed that he was the reincarnation of a Jewish prophet, Elijah.

Strange…a Jewish prophet killing six million Jews? He should have killed Germans. But the problem was, he had the same stupid idea: that the Nordic German race is the superiormost race; it is born just to conquer the world. Other races are subhuman. That was the clash. Two 'chosen' races cannot live together. Their egos continuously get into conflict.

All these religions say there is only one God – and one God creates three hundred religions just to fight with each other? This God must be mad, if he exists at all.

I feel it is better that we should trust Friedrich Nietzsche's declaration that he is dead, because to be dead is better than to be mad. At least you died in full sanity.

My feeling is he committed suicide, seeing the situation and what a mess he had created.

In India, God created the world – this is specially for the self-styled, cultured city of Poona. God created the world, and the first thing he created was a woman. The woman that he created was his daughter, but he became infatuated; he wanted to rape his own daughter.

The woman became so afraid that she ran away and became a cow. Many women do that, it is nothing special. God, seeing that the woman had become a cow, immediately became a bull! And this is how the woman went on slipping from one body into another body, and God went on running after her, becoming another male of another species. That's how all the species were created. This is the great religion of the Hindus – a cultured race, the most ancient religious people of the world.

Even their God is a *gunda,* a hooligan, a rapist – and they call themselves cultured. These self-styled, so-called cultured people should look into their own scriptures, and they will be surprised.

One of their reincarnations of God is Parashuram, perhaps the most violent man in the whole history of mankind. His father was a Hindu seer – I sometimes beat my head: a Hindu seer, and in his old age still jealous about his beautiful wife.

There is no evidence for it, but the Hindus believe that the moon is a god, the sun is a god.

The old seer, the father of Parashuram... I don't know what his original name was, because *parshu* is a special kind of sword, very heavy, not as long as a sword, almost half the size, but broad enough. A single blow...it is so heavy that a single blow is enough to take your head off. I don't know what his original name was, but because he continuously carried a parshu, he became Parashuram.

His father one day called him, saying, "I suspect your mother. She is having a love affair with the god of the moon. When I go to take my bath early in the morning at three o'clock, the moon comes and makes love to your mother. I cannot tolerate it. I have always found whenever I go to the river, the moon hides in the clouds. I know perfectly well where he has gone."

Is it just idiots that you call seers? – they don't even know that if a moon falls in love with a woman, the woman will be finished. You will not find even a fragment of the woman. It is so big – it is one eighth of the planet earth – that no woman can make love to one that size. How is she going to find where his mouth is? where his hands are? And how can the moon enter in the small hut of the Hindu seer?

But still nobody has condemned Parashuram's father, that he was a blind man, utterly blind – and you call him a seer? He was so blind with jealousy, so enraged that he was almost insane. The reality was that he had married a young woman, very beautiful, and he was old and finished.

He ordered Parashuram, "You go, this is the order of your father" – and obedience is the greatest religion – "cut the head of your mother and bring it before me."

Parashuram is thought to be one of the reincarnations of God, and even he could not see that it was all nonsense. "How can the moon come when I am always here? You go to the river, and if the moon comes I will chop his head." But he did not say anything. He simply went inside the hut and cut the head of the poor woman and brought it.

The father was absolutely satisfied. And because he obediently went – even to cut the head of the mother, without even asking a single question – Hindus have accepted him as one of the incarnations of God, pure obedience.

Pure obedience, or pure slavery?

Pure obedience, or pure stupidity?

And because the moon and the sun are thought by the Hindus, to belong to the race of the *kshatriyas*, the warriors – Hindus cannot think without bringing in their caste system – so the *surya*, the sun, and the moon are both warriors, kshatriyas, lower than the brahmins. Parashuram was a brahmin, and he was so angry with the moon that he decided to kill all the warriors of the country. And this man is thought to be an incarnation of God. What did the other warriors of the country have to do with his mother, or his father?

And the strangest story is... He was a man of tremendous power. *Sixteen* times he destroyed the whole race of the warriors of this country. His whole life was wasted in killing and killing, continuously killing single-handedly sixteen times.

From where then have the kshatriyas come? He has destroyed them all sixteen times. Do you need to destroy them sixteen times? One time would have been enough: all the kshatriyas are killed. How do you manage to get them killed sixteen times? That is another vulgar story of Hinduism.

Hinduism allows its seers... On the one hand they are talking about celibacy, promoting celibacy as the highest religion, and on the other hand they allow the seers, the great saints: "If any woman comes to you and asks for a child from you, you cannot refuse."

That's how...because Parashuram did not kill the women. The seers must have been having a jolly good life! Thousands of women, wives of kings, daughters of kings were coming to them on their own accord, praying to be given a child by them.

What kind of seers...?

These seers seem to be male prostitutes, and they are giving free service to all and sundry. The country is so big. Parashuram may be killing in the south; in the north new children are born. By the time he is finished in the south, again a new race of warriors has arisen. By the time he finishes the north, the east, the west, his whole life... And there were so many seers, and perhaps many were pretending to be seers. Such a good chance!

These vulgarities, these obscenities nobody mentions, because they will destroy the ego of the country, that this is the country of the pious, of the spiritual, of the religious. Can you think that these seers can be called seers, they have seen the truth, they have become awakened?

And Parashuram himself is the most unconscious human being. Without any reason, just because the Hindus believe that the moon is a warrior, all warriors should be killed. And he must have made the whole country into a whorehouse, but still he is recognized as one of the incarnations of God.

In India, for almost ten thousand years... That is the calculation of the modern scientists. Christians never believed in ten thousand years because of their Bible; their Bible says God created the world only four thousand years before Jesus was born. That means only six thousand years from this moment. So everything has to be put in the framework of six thousand years. They decided that the Rigveda was written five thousand years ago; they cannot go beyond that.

But scholars have found that the Rigveda was written ninety thousand years ago – with solid evidence, which cannot be argued against. The Rigveda describes a certain constellation of the stars which only happened ninety thousand years ago. Unless the people who had been writing the Rigveda had seen the constellation – it has not happened again... It is absolutely certain that these people watched the constellation, and they have described it in minute detail in the Rigveda. But ninety thousand years is a long story and nothing is written about it.

Most probably *satipratha* – when a husband dies the wife should also jump in the funeral pyre – is as old as the Rigveda. If the Rigveda is five thousand years old, then satipratha is five thousand years old; if it is ninety thousand years old, sati is ninety thousand years old. In ninety thousand years, how many million women – sometimes very young, just married a week before, or maybe a day before, even if the marriage is not consummated...? In India, even children used to be married – even now they are married, against the constitution and the law – even children who were in the mother's womb were married. Just two friends would decide that, "If my wife gets a boy and your wife gets a daughter, or vice versa, they will be married." This is decided. The marriage is final. You cannot send a one-day-old or a one-year-old girl to the husband's house, but she is married. The marriage may never be consummated. The girl may be five years old and the husband may die. In fact there was more possibility of dying than being alive.

In ancient India, up to the beginning of this century, out of ten boys, nine would die. And if you are marrying children – the wife has not even seen her husband, but if he dies she has to jump in the funeral pyre.

I have been asking the shankaracharyas, the Hindu religious leaders, "If you think that it is a great spiritual phenomenon that the wife should die, should jump alive in the funeral pyre, why has no man done such a spiritual act?" Only women are to be spiritual, and men have to be bulls?

I have seen with my own eyes live women burning. It is such a horrible experience to see, because a living woman tries to run out of the funeral pyre – she is alive – and brahmins are standing all around with big torches to force her back into it. So that it is not seen, much purified butter, ghee, is poured on the funeral pyre. It becomes almost a cloud of smoke, and you cannot see what is happening inside the cloud. Inside the cloud of smoke are standing the priests with burning torches to push the woman back into the funeral pyre, and outside there is so much music, bands, noise, that nobody can hear the woman praying, screaming, shouting "Help me! Save me!" Nobody can hear. All around a ceremony is going on, because one woman has become spiritual.

I have been asking; nobody has answered me. I am perhaps the only man in the world who has not been answered on a single point.

I have been to so many shankaracharyas – there are eight, one for each direction. "If spirituality is so easy, just jumping into a funeral pyre, why has not man attained such spirituality?" And they are dumb – they don't have any answer. They have only one answer: to condemn me.

But the fact is clear, it is a male chauvinist country. All religions are male chauvinist, against women.

I have been in such horrible nightmarish situations. I have seen women burning and I have seen how they have managed it. One layer of great music, loud music; another layer, another circle inside it, with great reciting of Vedic scriptures; then the third layer, which is almost hidden in the cloud that the purified butter has produced – the priests. Should I call them priests? – they are the butchers. They are standing around the funeral pyre with burning torches forcing the woman who is running here and there, trying to find a way out. But there is no possibility.

This you call spirituality, forcibly killing a woman? But the reason is, man's possessiveness.

All religions are male chauvinistic, they are in favor of the man. The man wants to possess the wife while he is alive and he wants to possess her even when he is dead. He will not leave her alone to have some love affair with anybody else.

But as far as man is concerned, I have seen a wife

burning on her funeral pyre and the husband talking with people: "Do you have some idea of where to find a beautiful girl? I want to marry again" – just on the spot. They cannot even wait for two, three days. At least let the fire disappear, let the woman's body be burned completely. No, exactly at the funeral pyre, around it, people are sitting and discussing which girl will be suitable for the person. And the person may be old, it does not matter; a fifty-year-old may marry a girl of sixteen years of age.

The crimes against humanity are immense.

The crimes against nature… All the people who have been eating meat don't think for a single moment it is coming from a living being. Just for your taste you are ready to kill anybody. What is wrong about cannibals?

One man who was caught by cannibals but somehow escaped told me, "I had to eat breakfast because I am too thin. That's why I could manage to escape – they were feeding me and preparing me." Unless he becomes fat enough, there is no point in making a soup of him. That gave him enough time, but meanwhile he had to eat human meat, human flesh, and he told me, "I hate to admit it, but I cannot resist telling you the truth: it is the most delicious thing in the world."

Just because it is delicious, will you start eating human beings?

Just because it is delicious, you have been eating all kinds of animals – that's what the Bible allows you – birds in the sky, fish in the waters, animals in the forests. You are the only king of this whole nature: conquer, eat, enjoy. Just destroying the animals…! Finally, man had to start eating fruits as well because there were not enough animals.

There was a stage when man was a hunter. There were no settlements, people were continuously moving wherever the animals were moving. The animals were escaping from human beings. But when they found a scarcity of animals they started eating fruits, they started cultivating. For cultivation they had to cut trees – trees which grow in two hundred years or three hundred years. There are trees which take four thousand years to grow. They destroyed those beautiful species forever. And they continued to produce more and more population, and the need for more land forced them to cut more trees. Without trees the oxygen layer on the earth has fallen very much. We are living on the minimum.

There are strange catastrophes which will be called "natural," but they are not natural. For example, in Nepal – it is one of the poorest countries in the world – they have sold their trees to the Soviet Union. Millions of trees have been cut, and the contract still remains intact for the coming thirty years. The Soviet Union does not use axes to cut the trees, it has very refined technology. In a day it can cut thousands of trees. Within seconds, trees which have grown in three hundred years will fall down. The whole of the Himalayas surrounding Nepal have become naked of foliage, and because of that... The Ganges used to flow slowly because there were so many trees; they were a kind of hindrance. The Ganges was coming slowly, slowly, slowly, to meet the ocean in Bangladesh. Now there are no trees, the floods come with such tremendous speed that this year three fourths of Bangladesh was flooded. It is also a poor country. Millions of people died. Millions of houses were simply washed into the ocean.

Now, Bangladesh cannot do anything, and if you ask

Nepal, the king says, "My people are so poor. We don't have anything to sell. We have only trees, and I have to feed my people. It is not my problem what happens to Bangladesh."

Next year, perhaps the whole of Bangladesh will have gone into the ocean. And how long can Nepal live by selling its trees? In thirty years the Soviet Union will have taken every single tree out of Nepal. Then comes a great danger: if the eternal ice of the Himalayas starts melting. The trees were shading the snows from the sunrays – thick trees, big trees – and the snow in the Himalayas has never melted, it has been there since eternity. But now there are chances you will see a tremendous flood – and there is no Noah's Ark available anymore.

If the Himalayas melt, all the oceans around the world will rise by up to forty feet. Bombay will be drowned, New York will be drowned; they will all become ocean. Cars will not be of any help – boats. You cannot survive if all the oceans rise forty feet higher – and you will call it a "natural" catastrophe...?

I don't call it a natural catastrophe. I call it a man-manufactured catastrophe.

The religious leaders have not been doing anything to prevent all these catastrophes. The population goes on growing; lands become poorer and poorer because they have been cultivated for thousands of years and they have not been nourished.

I told you that just at the beginning of this century, nine children were dying out of ten. Now the situation is just the opposite: one child dies out of ten, nine children go on living, because of medical facilities. We have disturbed the whole ecology of the earth.

Who is responsible?

Certainly religious people, who should have warned humanity not to increase the population...but they all are in favor of more population. Even Indian religious heads are against population control, because they need more and more members in their organizations, in their churches. They are not concerned at all about the whole planet earth getting destroyed by our own hands. And these so-called religious people are such a lying gang of criminals.

Just today I received my birth chart from one newspaper, *Veer Arjun*. The astrologer is K. A. Dube Padmesh. From where has this man got it? I don't know my own birth chart. Nobody knows my birth chart. It has never been made. I was born in such a small village where there was no airport, no railway station, no buses reaching to the village, no roads – just two hundred simple villagers living. There was not any astrologer to make my birth chart. From where these so-called religious people...?

Astrology is part of the Hindu religion. From their own imagination they managed to make my chart. I have come across many charts – during these thirty years I have come across at least two dozen birth charts. They are invented by astrologers – I don't know from where – and then they interpret them. They invent the chart and then they interpret the chart. They don't even ask me. I don't have a birth chart.

But lying has penetrated the religious people so deeply and fundamentally.... What do the great stars have to do with an ordinary human being like me? All these stars are deciding my fate? I am not a puppet.

ONE SEED MAKES THE WHOLE EARTH GREEN

Once it happened in Jaipur, the capital of Rajasthan.... They used to have one of the very famous astrologers – astrologer to the king of Rajasthan. I was staying with the king. He called his astrologer, because I had no birth chart. The astrologer said, "There is no problem. I will read your hands."

The king told me, "This is a very costly man, but I will pay, don't be worried."

I said, "No. Leave it up to me. Don't interfere, just keep quiet."

He used to get one thousand rupees for one reading. He did the reading and then he waited for the one thousand rupees.

I said, "You are a great man of predictions. You know everything, but you don't know I am not going to pay!"

He said, "What?"

I said, "Yes, you wasted my time. *You* have to pay me."

He said, "This is too much. If you don't want to pay it is okay, I will go. But you are asking *me* to pay...?"

I said, "You have been holding my hand. I don't allow anybody to hold my hand. You have been talking nonsense and wasting my time."

I told the king of Rajasthan, "Tell this man he should put one thousand rupees here."

The king said, "He is a poor brahmin. I will give you one thousand rupees."

I said, "It does not matter. Because money is money... you put one thousand rupees here."

The king had to put one thousand rupees. I returned it to him. I said, "I don't need it for the time being. Sometime I may need it – with interest. You called this idiot and you told me, 'He is the great astrologer in my kingdom....'"

But religion has been lying in every possible way, exploiting people in every possible way. Unless religion dies, the true authentic religiousness cannot be born.

A little biographical note before I talk about the sutras Maneesha has brought. These sutras belong to the world of Zen. To me, Zen is the only authentic religiousness. It has nothing to do with Buddhism, it has nothing to do with Taoism. In fact it is a rebellion against the traditions of Buddhism and of Taoism. But it has carried the essential message of Buddha. It has discarded all that was mere commentary. It has cut all rubbish out of the way. It is the very essence of Buddha's experience – and that is also the experience of Lao Tzu, of Tao.

Zen is paving the path for the future humanity of one religiousness.

Zen is the only authentic gold that has come out of the whole past of humanity.

My love for it is not in vain.

I am trying to help you understand Zen for a particular purpose – because you are going to be the new man, you are going to create a new humanity, a new world, which essentially is growing towards buddhahood.

The buddha is nothing to do with Gautam the Buddha; the buddha is your very nature. It means, the awakening. You are unconscious. Deep underneath your unconsciousness there is hidden a flame of awareness, alertness. That flame is *buddha-dharma,* that is your very nature. You don't have to go anywhere to find it, you have to go inwards. No church, no organization, no religion…just a quality of religiousness.

And what is the quality of religiousness? The quality of

religiousness is to be centered in your witnessing being. Out of that witnessing a great awareness arises in you; the spring comes to your life and thousands of flowers of compassion, of love, of blissfulness. All around the fragrance of the ultimate surrounds you.

This is a small biographical note about Fuketsu, a Zen master.

Fuketsu (who was born in 896 and died in 973) first studied the Confucian classics.

Confucius was not a religious man, Confucius was just a moralist. Confucius was just a parallel to Karl Marx. It is not a coincidence that China has turned communist, because Confucian ideology paved the way. All that matters is right manners, right morality, right etiquette; no mention of spirituality, only social behavior; no mention of your individual depth. Confucius was one of the most confused men that has been born in the world.

Fuketsu first studied the Confucian classics, then became a priest. Later he learned from Kyōsei, the disciple of Seppō, and then finally he went to Nan In – one of the greatest Zen masters – *through whom he realized his enlightenment.*

Studying Confucian classics, he must have understood that Confucius deals only with the outer world, society, social manners. "This is not my search; I want to know myself. I want to know what is my being, in what way my roots are connected with the cosmos; from where comes my life, and to where it goes; whether there is something more than the body and the materials that constitute the body-mind system, or there is nothing except this body, which will be put on a funeral pyre, or in a grave, and will disintegrate into the earth, into its basic elements."

I am reminded of a disciple of Confucius. He asked Confucius, "I have heard so much about Lao Tzu...." They were contemporaries. Sometimes it happens almost like a chain-reaction....

In China there was Confucius, a great thinker but materialist; Lao Tzu, a great buddha; Chuang Tzu, Lieh Tzu. In India there were Gautam Buddha, Mahavira, and six others whose scriptures have been burnt by the Hindus, whose statues have been destroyed; just their names remain in the words of Buddha, or in the words of Mahavira. At the same time, in Greece there were Socrates, Heraclitus, Dionysius, Diogenes. Suddenly the whole world was afire with a new insight.

Confucius' disciple asked him, "You must have heard about Lao Tzu. He talks about a space inside where there is only peace and nothing else, utter silence and no disturbance. Will you teach me how to enter inside?"

Confucius was very angry. He said, "Stop all this nonsense. Learn the morality, the virtue, avoid the sins, behave like a gentleman. Learn the manners of the society. As far as your inner world is concerned, when you die you will have eternity for that in the grave. You can search and meditate and find what is inside. But right now, don't waste my time." That was his attitude.

But, by and by, many people talked about Lao Tzu. Finally Confucius gathered courage. He was very much afraid, because the stories that he had heard about Lao Tzu were so strange: "The man can do anything. He rides on a buffalo, facing backwards – a dangerous fellow."

But the more he wanted to avoid him, the more he became interested. That's how the human mind functions. Whatever you want to avoid you will come across

ONE SEED MAKES THE WHOLE EARTH GREEN

again and again. You will become enchanted. Finally he decided to meet him.

Lao Tzu was not far away, just outside the capital in the mountains in a cave. Confucius went there. He stopped his disciples who had followed him outside the cave, because he was afraid: "That man can do anything. He may hit me, and I don't want my disciples to see what happens to me." He said, "I will tell you. First let me go and encounter that man."

Lao Tzu was sitting in the deep cave in darkness, very silently. He did not bother at all that Confucius had come. He did not say hello to him, he did not say, "Sit down, please." He did not take any notice.

Confucius said, "This is strange. At least you should behave like a gentleman."

Lao Tzu said, "I thought that you would not have the guts to enter into my cave. Here we don't teach morality or gentlemanship. Here we teach how to die and get resurrected. Are you ready?" – looking into his eyes – and Lao Tzu pulled his sword.

Confucius said, "Please forgive me. I will never again come in your cave!" – perspiring, and the cave was very cool.

He came out and he told his disciples, "This man is dangerous. He is a dragon. He would have killed me." He did not understand Lao Tzu at all. He was not talking about ordinary death, he was talking about the death of the ego. And unless the ego dies, you are not your authentic self, you are not your original face. Confucius missed.

Fuketsu must have understood that "These classics are

not going to help me." He dropped Confucius and became a priest.

But becoming a priest, worshipping statues and doing rituals, does not help either. The statue is as much outside you as anybody else; it does not lead you inwards. All your prayers, all your rituals are based on a fundamental lie: the existence of God.

Finally he became disappointed with being a priest also. He came to Kyōsei, a Zen master, the disciple of Seppō, another great Zen master.

Kyōsei told him, "Nan In is still alive. When the great buddha is still alive, why bother about small people like me? I can teach you, I can help you, but my first help is: go to Nan In. I am just a small pond, he is the very ocean. You cannot see the further shore."

This is the beauty of Zen. No other religion will send anybody to another master. There is conflict, competition. Everybody wants to be the greatest one. If somebody has come, he will grab him, he will not allow him to go anywhere else. He will take a promise: "I surrender to you."

Zen never wants anybody to surrender. No contract!

Out of your freedom you come.

Out of your freedom you learn.

Out of your freedom you grow.

Out of your freedom is going to happen your enlightenment. This is not an exception, it is almost the rule. If a master looks into the eyes of a disciple, he can see who will be the right master for this man, and he will direct him to the right man.

And when a man like Nan In is alive, why not take the chance and the opportunity? It happens very rarely over the centuries. Centuries pass, then only you come across a man like Nan In.

So he went to Nan In, through whom he realized his enlightenment.

This is just a biographical note on Fuketsu.

He stayed with Nan In for six years, and then became head of the temple at Mount Fuketsu, where he remained for seven years.

It has been a tradition in the past in Japan: if a master makes a temple on a mountain, and he is enlightened, the emperor names the mountain according to the name of the master. Because Fuketsu has made a new monastery, a new opening, a new space for the seekers to come, the emperor of Japan named the mountain Fuketsu.

He was Rinzai's great-grandson in the dharma lineage.

The sutra:

Our Beloved Master,
Once, a monk asked Fuketsu, "What is the buddha?"
Fuketsu replied, "The bamboo whips of Mount Jorin."

You will be surprised by the answer, but what he is saying is not exactly what he means. When he said, *"The bamboo whips of Mount Jorin"* – Mount Jorin was just in front of Mount Fuketsu – at that moment a breeze must have passed through the bamboos on Mount Jorin and the bamboos must have been making sounds, whipping each other, dancing in the wind, in the sun.

At *this* moment, Fuketsu was asked by a monk,
"What is the buddha?"

Fuketsu replied, "This very moment…to be alert and aware *this* very moment is to be a buddha.

Just see the bamboos whipping on Mount Jorin...."

Zen trusts only in this moment. Zen cannot talk about some Gautam the Buddha hundreds of years past. When the bamboo buddhas are dancing in the air, making great celebrating noises, it is enough to indicate to the reality, this moment. That was Buddha's essential message: to live in the moment, never in the past, never in the future. To live in the moment...and you have become a buddha. To be here and now, and you are a buddha.

Another monk then asked, "What is the buddha?"
because he could not understand what was going on. The man was asking, *"What is the buddha?"* – and you are talking about the bamboos.

So the other monk asked again,
"What is the buddha?"
Fuketsu answered, "What is not the buddha?"
This is a tremendous answer:
"What is not the buddha?"
Buddha is the very nature of existence. From the smallest grassleaf to the biggest star, everything is intrinsically, potentially, a buddha.

Some buddhas are asleep, there is no harm in it.

Some buddhas have awakened, there is no glory in it.

Just take care, when you are a sleeping buddha – don't snore, because that disturbs other sleeping buddhas. Not to disturb anybody, not to interfere in anybody's territory – that is the only virtue I know of.

There is not much difference.... I was asleep yesterday, today I am awake. Today you are asleep, tomorrow you may be awake – or perhaps *today*.

The buddha is our intrinsic nature, hence Fuketsu has made one of the most significant statements:

"What is not *the buddha?* You tell me.
"You ask me, What is the buddha? Are you mad? Life itself is buddha. Existence itself is buddha."

Yes, buddhas are found in two categories: a few are asleep, may be tired, tired of many many life circles, many many births, many many deaths, resting. But a few have rested enough. They are tired of rest, so they get up. But there is no essential difference: buddha awake, buddha asleep – both are buddhas.

Neither can sleep disturb your nature, nor can awakening enhance your nature. Yes, asleep you don't know who you are; awake, not only do you know who you are, you know the whole existence, its intrinsic quality – that of buddhahood. Once you become a buddha, suddenly the whole existence is a fire of awareness.

Great is the answer of Fuketsu:
"What is not *the buddha?"*

A third monk said to Fuketsu, "The Western Patriarch came bringing his message; I ask you to tell me it point-blank!"

He is asking about Bodhidharma. That is a constant question in the Zen world: Why has Bodhidharma come from India to China? What was his message?

At this, Fuketsu replied, "When one dog barks at nothing, a thousand monkeys really show their teeth."

A strange answer, but significant. He is saying, "Why are you bothered about these things? Bodhidharma came to China to bark!"

All the buddhas are doing exactly that: barking at sleeping people. Sleeping people means monkeys.

"When one dog barks at nothing…"

You must have seen dogs barking at nothing – great buddhas! Buddha's only message is nothingness, or, more point-blank, no-thingness. You are not a thing, you are not a commodity. You are beyond thingness. You are a light unto yourself.

"When one dog barks at nothing…"

Remember clearly that Zen accepts that dogs have as much buddha-nature as you have. Every living being… the very life is essentially hiding the buddha in itself.

"When one dog barks at nothing, a thousand monkeys really show their teeth."

When one Bodhidharma comes to China and barks, thousands of monkeys become Buddhists – but they have not understood the message. They laughed at Bodhidharma's barking at nothing; they enjoyed. For them, entertainment is enlightenment. Monkeys are after all monkeys.

But what he is saying, he is saying about humanity. If you are not a buddha, forget all about humanity. Of course you have the body of the human being, but inside, look at your mind – it is a monkey.

Only a buddha stops the monkey completely. Only a buddha lives in no-mind. And no-mind makes you authentically human, authentically existential, authentically part of the cosmos, of eternity. You disappear in the ocean of existence, and that is the greatest blessing, the greatest ecstasy.

On another occasion a monk asked, "What is the meaning of Bodhidharma's coming from the West?"

The same question.

Fuketsu said, "We know all the windings of the mountain stream, but not the mountain itself."

You have to note the fact. You can put the same question to the same master again and again, but you will never get the same answer again. A master responds to the moment spontaneously, he does not repeat from memory. His response is so pure….

Everything goes on changing, but *your* reaction remains the same. Response goes on changing with the changing flux of existence.

A master never reacts, he only responds.

So the question is the same, but Fuketsu's answer is totally different.

He says,

"We know all the windings of the mountain stream…"

He is sitting on Mount Fuketsu, and a mountain stream is winding around the mountain. It is a present moment. He shows the questioner,

"We know all the windings of the mountain stream, but not the mountain itself.

To know the mountain you will have to become the mountain. To know Bodhidharma you will have to become a Bodhidharma. There is no other way.

To know the Buddha you have to become a buddha. Being a Buddhist, you are monkeying, you are imitating. Monkeys are very great as far as imitation is concerned.

All the so-called religions are full of monkeys.

Christians are repeating Jesus; their famous classic is *Imitation of Christ*. Nobody thinks that 'imitation' is an ugly word. It is a very cherished classic of Christianity.

Buddhists are trying – imitating – to be a Buddha. But by imitating you can act like a buddha, but you cannot be a buddha.

If you want to be a buddha, forget all about Buddhas and

Christs and Krishnas. Just be yourself, enter into yourself, and you will find the buddha – not by being a Buddhist, but by just finding your authenticity, your innermost center. Don't be a monkey, ever.

I am reminded of a beautiful story.

A man used to sell Gandhi caps. Particularly at election time in India, Gandhi caps are very much in need. Everybody wants to prove that he is a Gandhian. The Gandhi cap is like a flag, showing to everybody that "I am a Gandhian. Vote for me."

A man used to make Gandhi caps for the election time, and he used to go from market to market selling the caps. It was a good business. The caps were in great demand.

One day, he was so tired coming back home. He himself was wearing a Gandhi cap, and in his bag he still had many caps left. He was thinking to go to another marketplace, but he was so tired that under a huge bodhi tree, the same tree under which Buddha became enlightened... That's why that tree is called a bodhi tree. It is named after Buddha. *Bodhi* means enlightenment.

It is a strange tree amongst all the trees; it can grow as huge as you want. Its branches after a certain length become so heavy they drop down. Because their weight is so great, to protect themselves the branches send new roots to the earth. When the new roots reach the earth, they have a new support. And each branch goes on sending new roots, so there are huge bodhi trees.

One exists in Adyar in the theosophical movement's world headquarters. It is so huge that ten thousand people can sit under it. The Theosophists used to have their meetings under the bodhi tree.

ONE SEED MAKES THE WHOLE EARTH GREEN

The man did not look at the tree, but it was full of monkeys. He was so tired, he just put his bag by his side and went to sleep. The monkeys watched. They could not resist the temptation of having a Gandhi cap. They came closer and they found that the man was fast asleep, so they pulled the bag open. Every monkey got one cap; only one monkey remained.

When the man had rested, he looked around. His bag was empty, and he could not see anybody. Then the monkeys started giggling. He looked up. He said, "My God! So many Gandhians! Now what to do?" Then suddenly he remembered that monkeys are imitators. So he took off his cap and threw it. All the monkeys took their caps off and threw them. He collected the caps and went back home.

The next year he fell sick at the time of the elections. He had prepared caps so he told his son to go to the marketplaces: "But remember one thing. There is on the way a very huge bodhi tree which is full of monkeys. And the shade is so cool...after miles of walking, one feels to rest. So I will tell you my experience, otherwise you will be in trouble. If it happens to you, remember, don't be worried: monkeys are imitators.

"If you want to sleep, go to sleep. If the monkeys take the caps, let them enjoy for a moment. When you wake up, don't be worried, just throw your cap and they will all throw their caps. Collect the caps and go home."

The boy said, "That's great." In fact, he was looking forward to enjoying the great moment.

Before going to the market – the father had rested when he was coming back – the boy thought, "Why not rest now and enjoy and then go to the market?" So with the full bag, he went to sleep. The monkeys came down, and when he woke up they were all wearing the caps.

The boy looked up. They all giggled. The boy knew the trick; he threw his cap. No monkey threw his cap; on the contrary, one monkey who had not got a cap came down and took his cap and went back up.

Not only had the boy's father told him, the monkeys had also been told by their fathers, "If such a thing happens, don't be deceived."

Bashō wrote:

Temple bells die out....

Have you ever listened to the temple bells slowly slowly dying out? The sound becomes less and less and less, or the echo in the valleys goes on dying, and then comes a great silence, greater than it was before the bells were rung.

> *Temple bells die out.*
> *The fragrant blossoms remain –*
> *a perfect evening!*

Bashō writes with such a golden touch.

You can see it exactly! You can hear the bell ringing and dying into deep silence. You can see the blossoms still remain, and the fragrance.

The silence deepens, the fragrance deepens...a perfect evening.

Haikus are, as I have told you, word pictures. Without painting, just through words, the haiku paints a picture, a very living picture. With paints the picture is dead. The poet's great art consists in painting a picture that will remain alive forever.

Temple bells die out. The fragrant blossoms remain – a perfect evening!

Maneesha has asked a question:

Our Beloved Master,
Are we born with an innate, inward propulsion towards self-realization?
Alternatively, is the nature of truth such that it attracts that which is of it? Or are there altogether different dynamics at play in regard to enlightenment?

Maneesha, both the things function together.

The magnet of your buddhahood pulls you inwards, and the thirst that is created out of disappointments in life makes you ready to search. You have looked all around and have not found anything. You have been thirsty, and thirsty, and thirsty, and everything has failed, all promises are broken.

Then a moment comes, you start looking inwards. "You have looked outside enough, just give a chance to the inner" – that idea arises automatically, and there is your innate buddha pulling you. And once you look inside, both start functioning together, moving closer to each other. Halfway they meet.

A Sufi saying is, "If you take one step towards truth, truth takes one thousand steps towards you."

No other dynamics is needed. All that is needed is a clarity about disappointment in the outside world, and an intelligence to remind you that you have not searched inwards. Just these two things are needed. A thirsty inquiry, and the buddha is sitting there like a great magnet pulling you towards him and also moving closer to you. The meeting is always in the middle.

I help you to go inside in search of your inner center. That is the center where you will meet the buddha. He will come out from the hidden treasure of your being to welcome you at the gate. The center of your being is the gate of the cosmos.

It is time for Sardar Gurudayal Singh. In fact, it is late!

Father Fungus has accumulated a huge gambling debt and needs some money fast. He has a bright idea for solving his problem. He wires up all the church seats with electricity.

The next Sunday, Father Fungus is blasting out his sermon when he stops and shouts, "All those who will give one hundred dollars towards the church charity fund, stand up!"

Fungus touches a button and twenty people spring to their feet.

"Good!" says Father Fungus. "Now, all those who want to give five hundred dollars, stand up!"

He touches another button and twenty more jump to their feet.

"Excellent!" says Fungus. "Now, all those who will give a thousand dollars, stand up!"

He throws the master switch, and fifteen visiting Scotsmen are electrocuted to death!

Father Fumble is visiting his central Oregonian flock and comes to the Sheep-Shaggers' farm near Fossil. He sees little Becky, the Sheep-Shaggers' daughter, playing in the front yard and goes over for a chat.

"Hello, my child," says Father Fumble. "May I speak to your father?"

"No," replies Becky, shaking her head. "He's in jail for molesting sheep."

"Really?" exclaims Father Fumble. "Then may I speak to your mother?"

"No," replies Becky, shaking her head. "She has been taken to the funny farm. She was talking to sheep."

"Really?" exclaims Fumble. "Then may I speak to your brother?"

"No," replies Becky. "He is at the university."

"How nice!" exclaims Fumble. "What is he studying?"

"He ain't studying nothing," replies Becky. "*They* are studying *him!*"

Muffin Snuffler, the White House cleaner, is polishing the floor in the Oval Office one day, when he looks up at George Washington's portrait and sees the lips moving.

Shocked and a little frightened, Muffin edges closer to the portrait and listens to America's hero speak.

"Bring me a horse!" commands Washington. "I am going to put this country in order!"

Muffin races out of the office and bumps straight into President George Bush. "Mister President, sir," he screams, "George Washington's portrait just spoke to me!"

"Don't be an idiot!" snaps Bush. "Pictures don't talk!" And he walks into the Oval Office and over to the painting. But before he reaches it, George Washington speaks again, "Hey, Muffin!" shouts Washington, "I told you to bring me a horse – not a donkey!"

Nivedano…

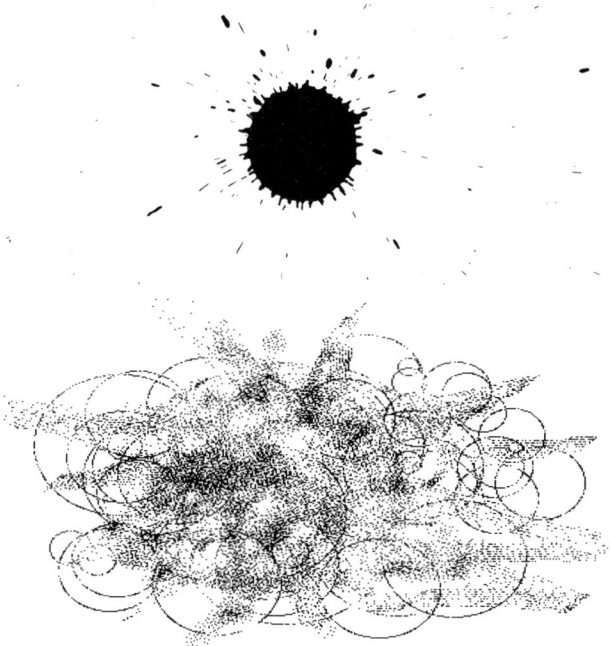

Nivedano…

Be silent…
Close your eyes…
Feel your bodies to be completely frozen.

This is the right moment to look inwards, with your total life energy, with your total consciousness, and with an urgency as if this is the last moment of your life.

Go as forcibly towards the center as an arrow, piercing all the layers of the body, mind, astral body.

Just go to the center.

As you come closer to the center, you are closer to the buddha.

As you come deeper into yourself, you are approaching your very being.

The moment you reach to the center, a great meeting happens.

You and buddha merge into each other, just as two lights merge into each other, and a great silence descends, and a tremendous joy arises in you.

Remember only one quality that buddha has. That quality is witnessing.

Whatever is happening, just be a witness, don't be identified.

You are not the body, you are not the mind, you are not the astral body.

You are not the silence, you are not all those flowers that are showering on you.

You are only a witness.

The witness is the very being of a buddha.

At this moment I am facing ten thousand buddhas.

Nivedano…

Help them to relax.

But remember to witness everything that is happening within you. Slowly slowly, you will feel a tremendous melting into the ocean of consciousness that surrounds you. Ten thousand buddhas are melting into an ocean of consciousness without any ripples.

Rejoice, cherish, this is the greatest moment of your life. You are the most fortunate people on the earth at this moment.

Collect as much fragrance of the inner, as many flowers of the invisible, as much juice of infinity, of the eternal, as much dance of existence as possible.

Nivedano…

Come back, but come back as buddhas, with great peace, silence, grace.

Sit down for a few moments just to remember the golden path that you have traveled. And just watch: every day the distance between you and the buddha is becoming less and less.

The day your center and your circumference become one, the day your day-to-day life is also an expression of your buddhahood – carrying water from the well, chopping wood for the winter – you will be a buddha in your meditation, you will be a buddha in all your activities. That day will be the greatest day in your millions of lives. That day you will be awakened from a coma, from a deep deep sleep for the first time.

For the first time you will know the beauty of existence, its truth, its splendor. Then all that remains for you is to share – share your joy, your ecstasy, with friends, with strangers.

Except the whole earth becomes filled with this festival of being a buddha, there is no hope for man.

But I trust in the intelligence of existence. You simply spread the fragrance. It will become a wildfire around the earth.

One single seed can make the whole earth green.

Okay, Maneesha?
Yes, Beloved Master.

One Wonders...

January 16, 1989

OUR BELOVED MASTER,
*Shojin Daishi came from India and said to Fuketsu,
"We learners have the three of the body, the four of
the mouth; I ask you to confess me!"
At this, Fuketsu snapped his fingers and said, "May
your sins disappear! May your sins disappear!"
On another occasion, a monk said to Fuketsu,
"People have collected like clouds;
please expound the dharma!"
Fuketsu replied, "People pursue a rabbit barefoot;
they eat the meat with their shoes on."
Another monk said to Fuketsu,
"Even without the practice of Zen,
may we certainly attain buddhahood?"
Fuketsu said, "The golden cock heralds the dawn;
the pitch barrel sends out a dark radiance."
At another time, a monk asked Fuketsu, "Both
speech and silence transgress. How can we not do so?"
Fuketsu replied: "I always remember the spring in
Kōnan, where the partridges sing:
how fragrant the countless flowers!"*

FRIENDS, I HAVE NEVER LAUGHED in my life as much as I have laughed this last week. Every day something hilarious happens.

Today I have received a message from the Dalit Elevation Republic Party, that I have to prove my sanity by a certificate from a psychologist. Only then are they ready to discuss matters with me.

Under my guidance, almost one hundred psychologists are working, and hundreds more come and go to learn meditation here. Whom should I ask for the certificate?

It reminded me.... When I graduated from the university I immediately went to the education minister of Madhya Pradesh. He was also the chancellor of the University of Sagar, where I had postgraduate degrees in psychology, in religion, in philosophy. Now that same person is the vice-president of India.

I went directly to him. I told his secretary, "I am going to meet the chancellor of my university, not the education minister, so don't come in between me and the chancellor. He knows me, he has been coming to the university every year for the convocation address. He has even addressed under my presidency the philosophical department of the University of Sagar. He knows me."

He informed the education minister, who called me in. He said, "What is the matter?"

I said, "I have passed from your university, and I have topped the whole university. This is the gold medal. I need a teaching job in any university."

He said, "You qualify absolutely. All the way you have been a first-class first, and finally you have topped the university, so you will get a place. And I know you personally, and I have always loved and respected you. Because you have been presiding over the meetings in the university where I was a guest speaker, I have heard you."

So he looked at my papers, the application, and then he said, "One thing is missing, your character certificate."

I said, "I know it. But do you want me to have a character certificate from someone to whom *I* cannot give a character certificate?"

He scratched his head. He said, "Perhaps you are right. What about your vice-chancellor? What about your head of the department of philosophy?"

I said, "You know perfectly well my vice-chancellor is a drunkard. Do you want me to get a certificate from a drunkard about my character? I cannot certify my vice-chancellor for *his* character.

"My head of the department of philosophy has never lived with his wife, has been living with another woman. He keeps his wife and children in Delhi just to avoid them, so that he can have all the women he wants. Do you want me to get a character certificate from him? I know him better; perhaps you don't know him that well."

He said, "It is a difficult problem."

I asked him point-blank, "Do you want to give me a character certificate? Do you think you are qualified? No politician in this country is qualified to give me a character certificate. Either you accept my application without the character certificate, or you refuse it.

"And I am here and you are asking for a character certificate. Look into my eyes! Look into my face! And do you have any understanding? Then don't ask foolish questions."

He immediately gave me an appointment in a college. I took the appointment order from his hand. He said, "This is not the right way, it has to go through the post."

I said, "When I am going to the college myself, why unnecessarily waste postage stamps?"

He said, "You are a strange fellow."

I said, "That's correct. But to be a strange fellow does not mean a man without character."

So I took the appointment order, and the next day I appeared in the college where he had appointed me. The principal could not believe it: "Just in one day…where did you get this appointment order?"

I said, "Directly from the education minister."

He said, "This is not routine. It should come through the post.".

I said, "Just because of this routine your whole bureaucracy is stagnant. I remember many cases…. One postcard traveled from Katni to Jabalpur, only eighty miles by road, in forty years. Do you want me to be appointed alive or dead?"

He looked at me, and he said, "That's true, I have also read many cases where a postcard has traveled for seventeen years, eighteen years."

So I said, "That's why I have brought it with me myself." But he was a little hesitant. I said, "You can phone the education minister in front of me. If you cannot trust me, you can phone the education minister."

He phoned the education minister, who said, "That appointment order is signed by me. You don't have to hesitate, give him the appointment!"

There are hundreds of psychoanalysts, psychologists, therapists, believers in other different schools of psychology, who have been here under me to learn meditation – because psychology itself has come to understand that it is incomplete. Without attaining a silent mind, all that you can do is analyze dreams. And analyzing dreams is not going to give you the essential being of the person.

Right now there are dozens of psychoanalysts, therapists present in this meeting – they have come from far away, well educated, trained, certified to practice psychoanalysis. But psychoanalysis itself is dying, because it has not cured a single person in the whole world. Twenty years of psychoanalysis…

Millions of dollars are being paid – because psychoanalysis is the most costly profession. But even they cannot claim that they have psychoanalyzed a single person completely. The whole effort of psychoanalysis is futile. They are simply scratching on the surface of the mind, looking into dreams.

Psychology does not believe in the soul of man. Psychology believes that mind is a by-product of the body, and the people who have not even inquired beyond the mind into the soul of man are making statements which are absolute lies. They have not inquired. The whole East has been concerned not with the mind, but with something beyond the mind.

Now they are becoming aware that threshing the mind for years you gain nothing. There must be something more, otherwise psychoanalysis and all other different schools of psychology are going to die. They are already dying.

One of the greatest psychiatrists of America, Dr. Weiss, for many years was thinking whether to say it or not – because it will create an uproar in the whole psychological movement around the world. He has been watching for years and seeing that psychoanalysis does not work. Unless something spiritual is added to it, it is on its deathbed.

But just now he gathered courage and wrote a book, *Many Lives, Many Masters*, and declared that psychoanalysis and all its different schools are in their last death throes. He has shocked the whole psychological movement around the world.

He is a graduate of Yale University and now one of the most respected American psychoanalysts – a psychiatrist, psycho-pharmacologist, writer of many books. A lifelong search has ended in the declaration that psychology is not enough.

The East has been saying this for almost ten thousand years. For what reasons was psychology not born in the East?

It is strange, because the East has been working on the inner world of man, and they did not develop a psychology. They did not bother about analyzing dreams, because they knew this is just treating the symptoms, and treating the symptoms does not cure the disease.

The disease is deeper than the mind, and unless you give man a clear perception of his being, of his eternal soul, nothing can help humanity. Only an experience of the eternity, the immortality of consciousness gives man wholeness – and I call this the only holiness also.

If these people whom I have been trying to help all my life... I have been in support of the oppressed, the suppressed, but they don't understand. Neither have they read any book of mine, nor have they ever come to listen to me.

I have six hundred and fifty books – perhaps nobody in the whole world has written six hundred and fifty books – translated into thirty-four languages of the world. And this uneducated, uncultured Dalit organization has some nerve to ask me that I should produce a certificate from a psychologist concerning my sanity.

England's greatest psychoanalyst, Ronnie Laing, has written just a few days ago. He has been sending his own patients, whom he could not cure in fourteen or sixteen years of work, to learn meditation. He wanted to come to be here for a few days. He wants to learn meditation – because mind is not enough; one needs something more of the eternity of existence.

Eighty-four of the most prominent psychoanalysts, painters, poets, philosophers of Italy have protested to the Italian government for refusing me entry into Italy. The same is the case in Holland, in Greece, in other countries.

Twenty-one countries have banned my entry into their territory. Never has there been an unarmed man... Just a word of truth creates fear in all those people who are living on lies.

Even the German parliament – I have never asked to enter Germany – without my asking, thinking that perhaps some day I may ask, has passed a law in the parliament that not only can I not enter into Germany, but my jet plane cannot be refueled at any German airport, because I might corrupt their morality, their religion, their culture – just in three weeks. A culture that has been propagated for two thousand years, a religion that has lived for two thousand years, is afraid of a single man. If your two thousand-year-old culture, morality, religion can be destroyed by a tourist in three weeks, then it is not worth having.

And if these people want to know, they can come to the ashram office. There are at least one thousand letters that were written to the American government when I was arrested there, from all kinds of prominent people around the world, condemning the criminal step of Ronald Reagan: arresting a man without any reason, without any arrest warrant. They had no evidence at all against me.

I never go out of my room. I am not concerned with anybody's morality and religion and civilization.

According to me, all these things have not yet happened. Man has yet to wait. Man is still living in the darkness of the barbarious past.

In three thousand years man has fought five thousand wars – and you call this man cultured? Just Genghis Khan, Tamerlane, Nadirshah – amongst these three they have killed one hundred million people.

The most cultured country, the most educated – which has created great philosophers like Kant, Hegel, Feuerbach, Karl Marx – is afraid of me. And this is the country of Adolf Hitler, who killed six million Jews in Germany in his gas chambers, and who killed in the second world war thirty million people. And they think they are civilized, they think they are cultured, they have a religion.

But if this Dalit organization wants, it can come to the office and look at all the protests that have been made to the president of America for arresting a mystic who has not committed any crime at all.

They fabricated, imagined, thirty-four charges against me, and not a single one had any truth in it. And the attorney general, Ed Meese, of America...

When they forced me to leave America, after my leaving, Ed Meese's representative admitted in a press conference, "He was innocent, he has not committed any crime." But the fundamentalist Christians – and Ronald Reagan was a fundamentalist Christian – did not want "this man" to be in the country.

One wonders, has man changed at all since Socrates, the greatest man of Greece, was poisoned? But the little man, the crowd of Greece, could not tolerate his height; they poisoned their own greatest genius. Since then Greece has never been the same. It committed suicide by poisoning Socrates. It is no longer a prominent country in the world. With Socrates it had been at the very peak of civilization.

The Jews killed Jesus, crucified him without any reason or rhyme, with no evidence of any crime. And since then the Jews have suffered immeasurably all around the world.

What crime had Jesus committed? What crime had al-Hillaj Mansoor committed? Mohammedans killed him, in a far more animalistic way than Jesus was crucified. They cut him piece by piece: feet, legs, thighs – they cut him piece by piece. And yet this man's crime was that he kept making the statement "Ana'l Haq" again and again. It means "I am the truth." That was the crime.

It seems that thinking is a crime in the eyes of the world.

One of the most important journalists, internationally well established, is M. V. Kamath. He has reviewed my books, and says that I am the greatest genius in the last part of this century. Mad people are never geniuses.

Another great journalist of India, the late editor of the *Illustrated Weekly of India,* has reviewed another book of mine on Friedrich Nietzsche's Zarathustra.

I am the only person who has commented on that book – because Adolf Hitler adulterated Friedrich Nietzsche's statements according to his own will. Whatever he wanted to use he had chosen out of Friedrich Nietzsche's work. And because of Adolf Hitler, Nietzsche became condemned. I had to pull Nietzsche out from Adolf Hitler's hands.

I have spoken on *Thus Spake Zarathustra.* Reviewing it, the editor of the *Illustrated Weekly* has compared me with Adi Shankara. He says in his review that "After Adi Shankara, there has never been anybody else of the same caliber and the same intelligence" – although I don't agree with him.

I would not like to be compared in any way to Adi Shankara. I accept Adi Shankara as one of the greatest philosophers, there is no doubt about it. But his philosophy and his lifestyle were contradictory; hence I don't want to be compared with Adi Shankara.

On the one hand he was saying, "We are all divine, we are all in our innermost being gods, the ultimate cosmic soul," and on the other hand he was accepting the Hindu caste system. He was saying that everybody is god in a hidden way. But what about the sudras? Even their shadow makes you dirty.

He was propounding the philosophy that the whole world outside you is illusory – but what about the sudras? They are the only real people it seems; everybody else is illusory.

One sudra touched Shankara when he had come to take a bath in the Ganges in Varanasi. It was early morning, still dark, and a man touched him intentionally. Shankara would not have detected anything because it was dark and he could not see the man, but the man himself said, "Wait! You will have to take another bath. I am a sudra."

Shankara freaked out. You don't expect a man of the intelligence of Shankara to freak out. He was so angry, so full of rage, he said, "Why have you touched me?"

The man said, "It is a question of philosophy. You say everything in the world is illusory. What about me? Is my body different from your body? Is my soul different from your soul? In your philosophy you are saying totally different things. Please practice them also."

So I understand the great compliment to me as the greatest genius after Adi Shankara, but still I will not agree to be compared with Adi Shankara. His philosophy and his lifestyle are contradictory.

The world-famous journalist and writer, Aubrey Menon, has written a book, *The New Mystics*. He has written about me in that book that when he encountered me in Bombay in a Cross Maidan meeting of almost fifty thousand people, he could not believe his eyes. He writes that he had been sitting in the front row when President Kennedy was speaking, but he could not feel anything. The speech was written by his secretary, it was not spontaneous. "It was ordinary, it did not touch anybody's heart. I came away utterly frustrated."

He had been in the rallies of Adolf Hitler, who was thought to be one of the greatest orators. But, he says, when he heard me, he heard a totally different kind of being.

Adolf Hitler was simply shouting slogans without any meaning, even nonsensical. He was telling the Germans, "All our miseries are because of the Jews." The fact was that the Jews were the richest people in Germany, and his eye was on their riches. "Kill the Jews and take all their money and all their factories and all their businesses!" And he convinced the so-called intellectuals of Germany – even Martin Heidegger, one of the most famous philosophers of this century – that Jews were the problem. "Because of the Jews, Germany is not able to conquer the whole world, so first finish the Jews."

Absolutely absurd.

Aubrey Menon writes, "I could not feel any conviction in what he was saying."

And when he heard me... I am absolutely spontaneous, simple. I don't know what word is going to come next, I don't know what I am going to say to you. I just face you and allow my being to be poured into your hearts. He felt it, and he could not believe that fifty thousand people were sitting so silently as if there was no one – pindrop silence. He says, "I understood the meaning of the phrase for the first time."

You can experience it here.

These ten thousand people can testify for my sanity. Raise both your hands if you think I am sane.

(With great laughter, everyone raises both hands.)
Thank you.
(More laughter and applause.)

Now the sutras. Maneesha has asked:

Our Beloved Master,
Shojin Daishi came from India and said to Fuketsu,
"We learners have the three of the body, the four of the mouth; I ask you to confess me!"

There are, according to Gautam Buddha, and according to all the mystics of the East – and particularly of India – three bodies. The one body you know is physical. Another body behind it is astral; it is made of pure light, hence it has no weight.

When you die only your physical body dies. The astral body takes your innermost being to another womb, unless you have become enlightened. If you become enlightened, then except your innermost center everything dies, and the center is for the first time released from the prison of the three bodies. It simply melts like ice in the oceanic consciousness of the universe. That is the ultimate freedom. We have called it *moksha,* we have called it *nirvana.* All those words mean ultimate freedom from all bondage of body and action, of mind and thinking, of feeling and emotions.

The third body is called the subtle body. It is completely

made of something like air. You can see the second body if you have the eyes of meditation. You can see the body of light; light is perceptible. But air is not perceptible even to meditators. The third body is the subtle body.

These are layers of protection.

Behind these three bodies is hidden your real being, your great splendor, your ultimate ecstasy.

And what are the four mouths? Gautam Buddha jokingly said, "Everybody has at least four mouths. You can have more, but everybody has at least four mouths." He means masks upon masks.

When you meet your boss you have a different face. When you meet your servant you don't have the same face. Just watch. When you meet your wife you have another face. When you meet your girlfriend you have another face.

You can watch from far away a couple walking towards you, and see whether they are married or not. The faces will show. The husband looks embarrassed, the wife is constantly being a detective. A beautiful woman passes by: the husband cannot look at her, the wife is watching.

It is said that a few people get out of bed in the morning, take their breakfast and go to their job; a few people get out of bed and go to their home.

When you see a man with a girlfriend, it is all joy. The same girlfriend will become a crucifixion.

I am reminded of a great psychologist who was surveying a madhouse. The superintendent took him inside. In a small room one man was just weeping and weeping, tears and tears, and was holding a photograph on his chest. It was such a miserable situation.

The psychoanalyst asked the superintendent, "What has happened to this man?"

The superintendent said, "He wanted to marry a woman – he has the photograph – but he could not marry her, and he has gone insane."

They moved to the second cell, and another man was hitting his head on the walls. The psychoanalyst asked, "What has happened to *this* man? Why is he hitting his head?"

The superintendent said, "You may not believe it: he married the same woman, and has gone mad!"

Buddha says everybody has masks, and unless you are freed of masks, you can never know your original face. The original face and the finding of it is the whole search of authentic religiousness. So, Buddha said, drop as many masks as possible. Everybody, the poorest of the poor, has at least four masks, and he goes on changing his face.

It starts even from childhood. You go to a school. If the teacher is not in the class, you watch the children. It is a chaos: books are being thrown, people are being beaten, they are writing anything they want on the blackboard. And the moment the teacher enters, absolute silence descends, everybody is looking at his book. They are not reading, but they are looking at the books.

What has happened?

Even small children…but we teach them. Mothers tell small babies, "I am your mother: smile." If the baby is not feeling to smile, why should she smile? You are teaching diplomacy. Slowly slowly the child learns, because he is dependent on the parents for everything. So when the mother comes, the child smiles. It is fake; he has no desire to smile. When the father comes, he smiles. It is fake.

We are creating frauds from the very childhood: "Respect your elders" – whether you respect them or not.

I was in constant trouble in my childhood. Anybody who was older, a distant relative – in India you don't know all your relatives – my father would tell me, "Touch his feet, he is a distant relative."

I would say, "I will not touch his feet unless I find something respectable in him."

So whenever any relative was to come, they would persuade me to go out, "because it is very embarrassing. We are saying to you, 'Respect the old man,' and you ask, 'Let us wait. Let me see something respectable. I will touch his feet – but without knowing, how do you expect me to be honest and truthful?'"

But these are not the qualities society respects. Smile, honor, obey – whether it is right or wrong does not matter. You will have respectability.

In the second world war, a professor in Germany, a professor of philosophy, was enrolled forcibly into the army. He resisted, he said, "You don't understand. I am a philosopher. I cannot kill people without any reason." But nobody listened to him.

They said, "We will teach him. Just let him come to the army quarters. Under a loaded gun he will come to his senses." But they had no idea of the man.

They brought him for the first parade on the ground in the early morning. The commander-in-chief ordered, "Left turn!" Everybody turned left, but the philosopher remained standing as he was.

The commander came to him and asked, "Why…? Are you deaf?"

He said, "No, but I had told you beforehand: I don't see any reason…why should I turn left?"

And then, finally, people turned left and right and went forward and backward, and finally came back to the same place. The professor said, "Aha! If they were all going to the same position again, then what is the point? I have been standing here all the time!"

The commander-in-chief thought, "This man is impossible."

He asked the general, "You have enrolled this man; I cannot cope with him. You give him some other job."

The general took him to the mess, and gave him a simple job: a pile of peas… He told the professor, "You sit down, and sort out the bigger peas on one side, and the smaller peas on the other side. I will come after one hour – and take care that the work is done."

After one hour he came back. The professor was sitting silently; the peas were exactly the same as when he had left. He said, "What happened?"

The professor said, "There are tremendous problems."

The general said, "What problems?"

The professor said, "There are big peas; okay, I can put them at this side. There are small peas, I can put them at that side. But there are some in between: where to put them? If I don't know where to put them I cannot sort it out.

"In fact," he said, "every pea is individual. I can make a line which will go miles away, the biggest pea, then the smaller, then the smaller, then the smaller. But this small mess will not do, I need a big ground!"

The general said, "Please, you go back to the university."

The man was simple and innocent and had no masks.

Buddha said everybody is a hypocrite. Everybody tries to show his face according to the expectations of the crowd. Everybody listens to the crowd, because the crowd never likes anybody who is a stranger, the crowd never likes anybody who is more intelligent.

In America I had my commune in Oregon, and I told the news media, "The people of Oregon are retarded." The politicians of Oregon were very angry, the governor was very angry, the attorney general was very angry. The supreme court of Oregon, the high court of Oregon – they were all angry.

I said, "Anger won't help. A survey is needed" – and an Oregon university took up the task. They came up with the conclusion: "He is right. The average Oregonian has only seven percent of intelligence functioning, and the average member of the commune has fourteen percent – double that of any Oregonian. You cannot start a case against the man. It is really a strange clarity of vision that he saw that the whole of Oregon is retarded. Seven percent is the intelligence of retarded people."

I have called the whole Indian parliament retarded, and the speaker of Lok Sabha wrote a letter to me, saying that "You have to apologize, you have insulted the parliament of the country."

I said, "I have not insulted anybody. First you get all the members of your parliament checked. If I am wrong, you can crucify me. And if I am right, then you all have to leave the parliament, and new elections will be needed."

He did not dare, because he knows… In the parliament people are throwing shoes at each other, using four-letter words which are not to be put on the record, shouting, wrestling with each other. He knows his parliament. He did not answer me, because that will be a strange phenomenon if by chance – and there is every chance – the whole parliament proves to be below seven percent. It will be a laughing matter for the whole world. It is better to keep quiet.

Buddha said that the society lives in a very fraudulent way. It lives in lies, it lives in imaginary consolations. It has so many faces. According to the place, according to the person, it changes its face. And he was telling this so that anybody who wants to be authentically religious drops all these masks.

You may not be aware that the word 'personality' comes from Greek. It means the mask. In Greek drama, in the ancient days, every actor used to have a mask. *Persona* means mask, and from persona has come the word personality. Unless you drop your personality you will not be able to find your individuality.

Individuality is given by existence; personality is imposed by the society. Personality is social convenience. Society cannot tolerate individuality, because individuality will not follow like a sheep. Individuality has the quality of the lion; the lion moves alone.

The sheep are always in the crowd, hoping that being in the crowd will feel cozy. Being in the crowd one feels more protected, secure. If somebody attacks, there is every possibility in a crowd to save yourself – but alone? Only the lions move alone.

And every one of you is born a lion, but the society goes on conditioning you, programming your mind as a sheep. It gives you a personality, a cozy personality, nice, very convenient, very obedient.

Society wants slaves, not people who are absolutely dedicated to freedom. Society wants slaves because all the vested interests want obedience.

The people who are in power, the people who have riches, the people who are the heads of religions, they all want one thing: you should not raise your head. You should live like a slave, pulled and pushed to this side and that side. You should not resist. You should not assert your being, your intelligence, your individuality.

This is the fear, the reason why twenty-one countries are preventing me from entering their territories: because I am in absolute favor of personalities dying and individualities being regained. That is real resurrection.

One great king, Prasenjita, contemporary to Gautam Buddha, had come to see Gautam Buddha for the first time. His wife had been a lay-disciple of Gautam Buddha for a long time before she was married to Prasenjita. She was a daughter of a greater king.

So when Gautam Buddha came to Prasenjita's capital, the wife said to the husband, "It does not look right that when a man like Gautam Buddha comes to your capital, you don't go to welcome him. *I* am going. He is sure to ask about you. What am I to say?"

The husband thought for a moment, and he said, "Okay, I am coming also. But because I am coming for the first time, I would like to give him some present. I have one very great diamond; even emperors are jealous because of that diamond. Buddha must appreciate it, so I will take the diamond."

The wife started laughing. She said, "Rather than the diamond, it will be better if you take a lotus flower from our big pond. To the Buddha the lotus flower is more beautiful. What will he do with the diamond? It will be an unnecessary burden."

He said, "I will take both and let us see who wins."

So he came on his golden chariot to the commune of Buddha, where ten thousand monks were sitting around him. Just before he was going to start his morning talk, the golden chariot of the king stopped, so he waited for the king to come in.

The king came in front of him, and first he offered Buddha the diamond. Buddha said, "Drop it!" It was very difficult for Prasenjita to drop his diamond – that was his very life! – but not to drop it also was difficult. Before ten thousand people Buddha had said it – "and you have offered the diamond so it no longer belongs to you."

He hesitated. Buddha said, "Drop it!" So he dropped the diamond, reluctantly, and offered the lotus flower with the other hand.

Buddha said, "Drop it!" Prasenjita thought, "Is this man crazy?" He dropped the lotus flower, and Buddha said, "Don't you listen? Drop it!"

He said, "Both my hands are empty. Now what do you want me to drop?"

At that moment, one of the oldest disciples of Buddha, Sariputra, said, "You don't understand. Buddha is not saying to drop the diamond, or to drop the flower. He is saying, 'Drop your personality. Drop that you are a king. Drop this mask, be just human, because through the mask it is impossible for me to approach you.'"

He had never thought about it. But a great silence, and

ten thousand people...and he fell spontaneously at the feet of Buddha.

Buddha said, "That's what I have been telling you: drop it. Now sit down. Be just human. Here nobody is an emperor and nobody is a beggar. Here everybody is himself. Just be yourself. This being an emperor can be taken away from you.

"Someday somebody will conquer your kingdom and you will be a beggar. This emperorhood is not your essential part. It can be stolen, it can be conquered, it can be destroyed. Better you yourself drop it – that is more manly – and just remain your authentic being."

Daishi had come to India to learn the teachings and the discipline of Gautam Buddha – long after Gautam Buddha, perhaps one thousand years after, looking for some awakened, enlightened person who can help him to understand what meditation is.

He was told that we have three bodies and four mouths. He could not understand. What three bodies, four mouths? He went back to Japan and reached the great Zen master Fuketsu, and asked him, "Please explain to me what is the meaning of this puzzling statement. I have only one body, one mouth."

At this, Fuketsu snapped his fingers –
just snapped his fingers –
and said, "May your sins disappear! May your sins disappear!"

This is the world of Zen, where an ordinary rationality is of no use. The man has asked something absolutely different, and Fuketsu answered in such a way that if you try to rationalize it you will be absolutely disappointed.

He did not answer on the surface – just on the surface he did not answer – but underneath the surface he answered.

I have to explain to you what was underground – that which cannot be said, but can be transferred. His statement, *"May your sins disappear!"* – just *(The Master snaps his fingers)* in a click...

The word sin in its origin, in its roots, means forgetfulness. It does not mean what Christians have been telling the world. It does not mean sin, it means forgetfulness.

And according to Gautam Buddha and Fuketsu that is the only problem. All other problems arise out of it, hence it can be called the original sin – forgetting yourself. And what is virtue? – remembering yourself. Being aware of your consciousness is virtue, and forgetting your consciousness and living an unconscious, robotlike life is the only sin.

He did not answer the question as far as language is concerned, but he is answering it in a far deeper way. He said, "Forget about three bodies, four mouths, just remember yourself. Drop forgetfulness, drop your sleep. Drop your spiritual slumber. Wake up!"

That is exactly the meaning of the word buddha, being awake.

"May your sins disappear!"
said Fuketsu, and repeated again,
"May your sins disappear!"
This will give you a taste of the way Zen works. It is very straight, but it is beyond your reason, your mind, your thoughts. It hits at the very center. Wake up, and all these problems and theorizations and ideologies will disappear. Why not cut the very root from where all the branches go on growing?

All the religions of the world, except Zen, have been trying to prune the leaves. Drop this sin, drop that sin – and how many sins are there? Drop greed, drop jealousy, drop envy, drop anger, drop violence... And by the time you have been able to drop one, one life may not be enough.

Gautam Buddha brought a rebellion into the world which still lives, aflame in the small stream of Zen masters. Just cut the very roots, don't bother about the foliage, because you should remember: if you cut one leaf, in response to your arrogance, violence to the tree, the tree will bring three leaves. That's how gardeners make trees thicker and thicker: by cutting their leaves, branches. You cut one branch, and two or three branches will sprout.

The same is true about man. You cut one sin, and three more sins will arise, because how can you cut greed separately? They are all together – your anger, your violence, your jealousy – they are all one, branches of one tree. Don't cut one; you will be cutting for lives together, and you will never come to the realization of the divine in existence. But if you cut from the roots, in a single blow, *this* very moment you can become a buddha. You don't have to become a Buddhist.

This is what is making the Buddhists go out of their senses.

Buddha is your essential core. It is not a question of conversion, it is a question of transformation. You have to go within yourself and cut the roots of all your darkness. Then suddenly a flame jumps up from your very center and fills your whole being, and slowly starts radiating around you, in your presence, in your eyes, in your gestures, in your grace, in your blissfulness.

The buddha is your birthright. It is not a question of imitating any buddha – there have been thousands – you need not imitate anyone. You have to find your own. You are carrying it from your very birth, perhaps for many lives, but you have never looked inwards.

The idea of waking up simply means waking up from your very center, so that you can see your authentic nature. The buddha is your nature. The moment you realize who you are, you will suddenly start dancing, singing, in a drunkenness which is divine, because you have found the source of all life, you have found the connection with the cosmic whole. You are no longer imprisoned in the body, you have found the door going out of the prison, and disappearing into existence.

This is called *nirvana*.

This is called becoming a god in your own right.

On another occasion, a monk said to Fuketsu, "People have collected like clouds; please expound the dharma!"
Fuketsu replied, "People pursue a rabbit barefoot; they eat the meat with their shoes on."

He was asked to tell something about the ultimate nature, which in Pali is called *dhamma*, in Sanskrit, *dharma*. It means exactly, your ultimate nature, your eternal nature.

The man was asking, "So many people have come, a great crowd like clouds has gathered around your temple, Fuketsu. You should teach the dharma."

Fuketsu replied in a way that means, "These people will not be able to understand dharma, they are so unconscious. These *people pursue a rabbit barefoot*."

He is trying to explain without saying directly that they are unconscious. Pursuing a rabbit barefoot is very unconscious. You may fall, you may trample on thorns. The rabbit will go zigzag in a forest; it is better to have your shoes on. But these unconscious people will pursue a rabbit barefoot, and

"they eat the meat with their shoes on."

In short, he is saying, "These people's actions are unconscious, they don't know what they are doing. They don't know who they are. They don't know from where they are coming. They don't know where they are going."

Everything about the masses is unconscious, but to tell them so hurts them. Rather than being thankful to you, that "You made me aware of my unconsciousness," they will be angry at you. They will think that you are insulting them.

A blind man was brought to Gautam Buddha. He was a great logician, and he defeated the whole village in a discussion about light. He insisted that there is no light, no sun, no stars, no moon – "because I don't have any experience of them."

People tried to convince him that there is light: "The whole village says so."

He said, "You will have to prove it. Bring the light, I want to touch it." Now, you cannot touch light, you cannot hold it in your fist.

He said, "Okay. Hit the light, I want to hear the sound." You cannot hit light either.

He said, "Okay. You bring the light, I want to smell it" – but light has no smell.

He said, "Then I want to taste it. These are the only

senses I have got." You cannot taste light, it has no taste.

The whole village was greatly upset. They know light is there, but this man is blind. "We don't want to say directly to him, 'You are blind' – but he is a great logician, we cannot defeat him."

Just then they heard that Gautam Buddha was to pass by their village. They said, "This is a great opportunity. We should take the blind man to Gautam Buddha. Perhaps he can convince him about light."

The blind man was brought by the villagers with great hope. But Buddha said to the villagers, "You are wrong. Seeing perfectly well that the man has no eyes, you are trying to convince him of light. He does not need a philosopher or a logician to teach him. I will give him my physical physician, and I hope his sight will be restored" – because he was not born blind.

Within six months his sight was restored. Buddha had moved to another place, leaving his personal physician with the blind man. The blind man looked around at the beautiful existence, the rainbows, the sun, the moon, the stars, the flowers and their colors. He could not believe that he had been missing all this beauty his whole life, and he had been unnecessarily arguing with the poor villagers, who didn't understand logic, but they were right.

He went to the place where Buddha had gone, dancing, and he fell at his feet saying, "If you had not come into my life, I would have remained always blind. Now I can see the greatest gift in life is the eyes" – because eighty percent of our experiences depend on the eyes, only twenty percent on the other senses.

A man without eyes immediately creates a great compassion in you. The same is not true when you come across a man who is deaf, or a man who has no legs. You feel pity, you feel sympathy, but not the same compassion as you feel when you see a blind man, because he is missing all the colors, all the rainbows, all the flowers, all the sunsets, all the sunrises, the whole starry sky; he is missing everything of beauty. The beautiful faces of men and women, the beautiful birds he is missing; that is the greatest calamity.

We are also blind in a sense, because we are not looking inwards.

In the East, particularly in this country, we have called it the third eye, which opens inwards just between your two eyebrows. When you go deeper in meditation both your eyes have to be closed, so no energy goes out and the whole energy concentrates just in the middle. And from there is the entry into the inner sky, which is far more beautiful, far more colorful, of tremendous ecstasy. The deeper you go in, the more you come close to the divine. When you have reached to the very source of your being, you have found the ultimate meaning and significance of life.

The masses are unconscious. According even to psychologists, if we divide our mind into ten parts, only one part has become conscious; nine parts underneath it are completely in darkness.

It is almost similar to an iceberg. Only one tenth of the iceberg shows above the surface of the sea; nine tenths is underneath. We are living at the very minimum, we don't know how to live at the optimum, and religion is nothing but to give you life in its totality, to help you to live at the optimum. When you can live as a divine being, why live like unconscious animals?

We have become human beings, but our innermost world is a complete darkness. We have never bothered even for a single moment to look inside.

Hence, Fuketsu said, "The masses cannot be taught, unless somebody becomes thirsty, unless somebody becomes frustrated with the outside world and wants to enter into the inner core, to explore the last resource. Outside he has not found anything; perhaps one thing is still left – that is inside."

When somebody comes not for teachings, not for knowledge, but for experience, then there is a possibility for a master to show you the path. Nobody can lead you to your inner being, nobody can go with you. You will have to go alone. But the master can show you the golden path.

Buddha says: I can show you the moon, but don't take my finger to be the moon. Drop the finger and look at the moon.

But this is the misfortune that has happened around the earth. Every religion is holding the finger! – somebody of Mohammed, somebody of Krishna, somebody of Buddha, somebody of Mahavira – and nobody is bothering where the finger points. The finger is not the religion. The teachings, the scriptures, they are all fingers, and people are worshipping scriptures.

I was staying in the Punjab in the house of Punjab state's Inspector General of Police. He was my host. When I went into my room I passed his temple. He had a small temple made in his vast bungalow. I looked in the temple, and there was *Guru Grantha Sahib*, the religious scripture of the Sikhs. It was early morning, so he had put a toothbrush and a tube of paste by the side of *Guru Grantha Sahib*.

I said, "My God, what are you doing?"

He said, "Just for *Guru Grantha Sahib*" – 'Sahib' makes the scripture almost look like a human being – "for his morning toothbrushing."

I said, "You are the I.G. of this whole state, and if you can do such a thing, what about the villagers? They may be giving him a bath, just a shower, feeding him food. They may have destroyed *Guru Grantha Sahib* long ago. You are a reasonable man, well educated, in a high post, and you are behaving like a villager!"

But this is the situation. If your foot touches *Srimad Bhagavadgita,* if you are a Hindu you will immediately touch the feet of *Bhagavadgita.* There are no feet! Scriptures have become reality, fingers have become the moon, for the unconscious masses.

Unless somebody on his own comes to a master… The crowds cannot be taught the deeper secrets of life. They are going to live in superstitions, in all kinds of consolations, but they will never know the nature of the great reality that you are.

On another occasion some monk asked Fuketsu,

"*Even without the practice of Zen…*"

Zen means *dhyan*, it means meditation. The word 'dhyan' is Sanskrit. When it moved to the Buddhist language, Pali, it became *zhan*. When it moved to China it became *chan.* When it moved to Japan it became Zen. Zen means dhyan; dhyan means a state of no-mind.

In English there is no parallel word. We use 'meditation' because there is no other word which comes even close. Meditation is not the right word. The moment you say meditation, immediately the idea arises: meditating on what? It is always objective. Concentration is objective, contemplation is objective, meditation is objective; dhyan is subjective. It is not meditating *on* something, it is simply moving inwards, silently, without any object in your vision.

Inside there is no object, only pure subjectivity – a silent lake of consciousness. And the deeper you go, the calmer and cooler and more blissful you become. When you reach to the deepest point in your being you have arrived home.

Fuketsu was asked,
"Even without the practice of Zen, may we certainly attain buddhahood?"

An absurd question. Without dhyan, without Zen, nobody can attain buddhahood. It is saying, in other words, "Can we reach inside without going inside?" It is absolutely nonsense, the question.

Fuketsu said,
"The golden cock heralds the dawn; the pitch barrel sends out a dark radiance."

Just as the golden cock heralds the dawn, meditation heralds the beginning of your buddhahood. Without meditation, you cannot taste anything of religion. You can believe, but belief is always of the ignorant.

I want you to understand absolutely: *Never* believe in anything. Experiment. Take the belief as a hypothesis but never as a certainty. Unless you experience, no belief can help you.

Can belief in water quench your thirst? Can belief in God herald the dawn? No belief system is of any help.

You have to go inwards, alone, as deep as possible.
Meditation is the very essence of all religions.
Everything else is mere commentary.

At another time, a monk asked Fuketsu, "Both speech and silence transgress. How can we not do so?"

It is especially a Zen question, especially a question for great meditators. When you arrive at your very being you experience something which is beyond words. Now there are only two possibilities. Either you use words, which don't justify your experience... They distort your experience, because the experience happened beyond words, far away, it cannot be dragged into ordinary human language.

So the one possibility is to speak. That transgresses the experience. The other possibility is to remain silent, but that too is not right. If you are silent, how are you going to share your experience with those who are all groping in the dark? The man is asking a very important thing.

When Gautam Buddha became enlightened, for seven days he remained silent, just thinking what to do. "If I speak, it is not exactly the truth, something is missed. And when you hear it, something more is missed because you will interpret it according to your mind, and you don't have that experience from which those words are coming. It is a transgression against truth.

"Should I remain silent?" Buddha thought. "But that seems to be very unkind, uncompassionate. So many people are searching, and I have found. At least I can help them in some way – if not through words, then through some devices. If not through words, then some other way has to be found to transmit the fragrance, the fire of my experience."

Finally, fortunately, he decided to speak. It would have been a tremendous loss to humanity if Gautam Buddha had not spoken. Although he always says, "Remember while you are reading my scriptures that the word is not the truth. It may indicate as a finger, but it is not the moon" – but who remembers?

People simply get knowledgeable by reading scriptures – rabbis, bishops, popes – but they are all knowledgeable; they don't have the experience. They have not known themselves, they have only believed. Belief prevents you from searching for the truth. Never stop at a belief. Stop only at an experience of your own.

Fuketsu replied: "I always remember the spring in Kōnan…"
where he used to live before he came to Mount Fuketsu. The mountain was renamed by the emperor of Japan according to the name of Fuketsu. It became Mount Fuketsu because he lived there, an enlightened light for millions to come and quench their thirst.

But before coming to this mountain, he used to live at another mountain.

He says:

"I always remember the spring in Kōnan, where the partridges sing; how fragrant the countless flowers!"

Do you see the point? He is not answering directly. Zen does not answer directly. It answers in a very poetic and indirect way.

He is saying:

"I can remember the spring in Kōnan, where the partridges sing; how fragrant the countless flowers!"

But you have never been to Kōnan, so you don't know what spring in Kōnan is, you don't know the flowers and the fragrance and the color and the beauty. Unless you go there, there is no way. "I cannot bring Kōnan and its spring and the flowers and the songs of the birds into my language. I can point you the way to Kōnan – go to Kōnan."

He is simply saying that the inner world has to be experienced. There comes a great spring...far greater than you have seen outside. There are flowers and fragrances of another world – a peace, a silence, a song, a dance that you have not known in the outside world. But the only way is: go in.

Issa wrote:

> *Pure simplicity*
> *marks the arrival of spring –*
> *a pale yellow sky.*

But you have to see it.

How many people look at the sky? I have been watching, standing by the side of the road: people are counting money on their fingers and they don't see that the sun is setting and is throwing such psychedelic colors all over the horizon – and they are counting money. I can see their lips moving. They are talking to somebody who is not present, and the sun is setting with such grandeur. How many people get up early to see the sunrise? How many people watch the immense hypnotic power of the fullmoon night?

Do you know, all those who have become enlightened have become enlightened on the fullmoon night, except Mahavira – just a single exception in the whole of

ONE SEED MAKES THE WHOLE EARTH GREEN

history? Strange...why on the fullmoon night? The ocean rises to greet the moon on the fullmoon night. More people go mad on the fullmoon night; hence the word 'lunatic'.

Lunatic means *luna*, luna means the moon – moonstruck. Lunatic means struck by the moon. More people commit suicide on the fullmoon night – four times more than any other time – more people murder on the fullmoon night. It has been a strange thing: why should it happen on a fullmoon night?

The full moon somehow makes you what you have been in some way repressing in yourself. If you have been repressing the desire to become enlightened, perhaps on the fullmoon night you will become enlightened. It exposes you. If you have been repressing the desire to commit suicide...

Psychologists say there is not a single man on the earth who has not at some time thought of committing suicide. Not that everybody commits it, but there are moments of trouble, anxiety, anguish, when one thinks it is better to finish it all. But the psychologists are not aware that this idea happens only on fullmoon nights.

The fullmoon night simply exposes you. If you are ready for enlightenment, if your meditations have ripened, you become enlightened. If you are ready to commit suicide and you have been somehow avoiding it – nobody wants to commit suicide, nobody wants to murder anybody, but the idea arises, and on the fullmoon night it is irresistible. Whatever you have been repressing, whatever you have been searching for is exposed.

But everything has to be your experience.

Pure simplicity marks the arrival of spring – a pale yellow sky.

You cannot go inwards if you are not finished with the outside world – its beauty, its treasure, its immense vastness. If you have not become acquainted with it, you will never think of going in, because the inner is vaster, the inner is bigger, the inner is more intelligent. The inner is pure wisdom. It is truth, it is beauty, it is godliness.

But first you should learn from the outside world. This is especially a Zen message. It is not against the outside world, it wants you to learn everything of the outside world so that you graduate from the outside to the inner.

Maneesha has asked a question:

Our Beloved Master,
Is enlightenment something like getting the punchline to the ultimate joke?

Right, Maneesha. It *is* the punchline of the ultimate joke.

This begins the time for Sardar Gurudayal Singh.

Percy and Porky Poke own a men's clothing shop in downtown L.A.

One day Buster Chubbs walks in and says, "I need a nice suit."

"Okay," smiles Porky, jumping up. "We have Paris suits, Italian suits, Mexican suits, all kinds and all styles, from every corner of the world. Modern, classical, new wave, formal, business – any kind of suit.

"You can get them in your favorite color," continues

ONE SEED MAKES THE WHOLE EARTH GREEN

Porky with his best sales pitch. "We have black, blue, grey, even orange – any color you want! What is your size?"

Buster is really impressed as he looks around the shop. "I think I am size forty-two," he says.

Porky proceeds to bring every size forty-two suit in the store and has Buster try each one. Every time Buster comes out in a different suit, Porky spins him around to look in the mirror – back to front, and front to back, spinning him this way and that, to see it from all the angles.

Half an hour later, Porky still cannot sell him a suit.

Then Percy walks up with the last remaining suit, says a few things to Buster, and Buster buys it.

When Buster leaves his shop, Percy turns to Porky and says, "See how easy it was? I sold it to him on the first try."

"Sure," says Porky, "but who made him dizzy?"

Boris Bagel gets invited to a fancy-dress masquerade and decides to go along dressed as Lucifer, the devil.

Unfortunately, on his way to the party, Boris gets lost and ends up walking into the middle of a Jimmy Bakker TV broadcast prayer meeting.

The good folks, watching preacher Jimmy Bakker give his fire and brimstone sermon, take one look at Boris in his devil outfit and start to scream and run for the doors.

In the panic, preacher Jimmy Bakker gets trampled to the floor and Boris, not realizing that he is the cause of the panic, goes over to help him up.

"Ah, Satan!" shouts Bakker, terrified. "I have been running this special Christian church for twenty years, but I want you to know I have really been on your side all along!"

Giovanni, the Italian, George, the Englishman, and Ivan, the terrible Russian, are working for the United Nations Army in Africa, when they are captured by cannibals.

Chief Boonga, the cannibal leader, tells the men that they can have one last request before they get thrown into the cooking pot.

"I-a want a plate of spaghetti!" says Giovanni.

"I would like a bottle of beer, please," says George.

"Just give me a kick in the ass," says Ivan.

Giovanni gets his spaghetti, George gets his beer, and Chief Boonga walks over to Ivan and gives him an enormous kick in the rear-end.

Immediately, Ivan pulls out a gun from his pocket, and shoots all the cannibals.

"I say!" exclaims George. "Jolly good show!"

"Mamma mia!" shouts Giovanni. "But what took-a you so long?"

"Well," explains Ivan, "being a good Russian, I could not attack until I was provoked!"

Nivedano…

ONE SEED MAKES THE WHOLE EARTH GREEN

Nivedano...

Be silent...close your eyes...
Feel your body to be completely frozen.

This is the right moment to look inwards. Collect your whole life energy, your total consciousness, and with a great urgency to reach to the center... One never knows, this may be the last moment of your life.

Deeper and deeper...just like an arrow passing through all the layers of body, mind.

As you come closer to the center, you are coming closer to the god....

As you come deeper, nearer, you are coming closer to the buddha hidden in you.

At this moment you are the most fortunate people on the earth, just because you are so close to your divine nature.

Remember only one thing, which is eternal in you, and that is the witnessing consciousness. Just witness everything.

The body is not you – witness.

The mind is not you – witness.

All the experiences that are happening to you – the great silence, the peace, the joy, the ecstasy, you are a witness. You remain always above and beyond.

This beyondness, this witnessing, is your real *buddha dharma,* your authentic nature, your divine individuality.

To make it clear, Nivedano…

Relax…

But keep on remembering that you are just a witness.

As the relaxation becomes more and more and more, you start melting like ice into a vast ocean of consciousness. Gautama the Buddha Auditorium, at this moment, has become an ocean of consciousness.

Feel…and collect the experience.

This is no belief, this is your own experience.

This is no finger, you have come to the moon.

And persuade the buddha to come along with you. He has to become your very life, your breathing, your heartbeat, your daily, ordinary activities.

Chopping the wood for the winter, carrying the water from the well, he should be with you. In fact, slowly slowly you will disappear, only buddha remains. That is the greatest day of your life, when only the buddha remains.

The word 'buddha' means the witness, the observer, the watcher – in essence, pure awareness. And pure awareness makes you one with the whole cosmos.

Collect as much experience as you can, and persuade the buddha to come along with you.

Nivedano…

Come back…but come back with grace, come back with blissfulness, come back as a buddha. And sit down for a few moments just to recollect where you have been, just to remember what golden path you have moved on.

Inch by inch the distance between your circumference

and the center is becoming less every day. The day your circumference and center become one, your actions and your consciousness become one, you have arrived home.

One single seed can make the whole earth green. A single buddha can make the whole world afire with a new consciousness and a new humanity.

You are the very hope of a world which is in great despair, in great anguish.

It is not only a question of your individuality, becoming a buddha, it is a question of saving this whole planet. This planet can be saved only by people who understand that every living being is divine.

To destroy anything is ugly and barbarious. Particularly to destroy life is absolutely disgusting, because if you cannot create life, you don't have any right to destroy it.

One seed makes the whole earth green.

Okay, Maneesha?
Yes, Beloved Master.

Books by Osho

Osho's discourses have been published in over six hundred books, many of which have been translated into several different languages, and most were originally published under the name of Bhagwan Shree Rajneesh. The following is a small selection of titles particularly related to the subject matter of this current volume.

MEDITATION: THE FIRST AND LAST FREEDOM

In this book, Osho has taken many different traditions and penetrated to the very essential core of each of their techniques. He does not just tell you what to do, he tells you why you are doing it and how the technique works to bring you to the essential element of awareness and witnessing. Many people have the technique but they don't really know what meditation is. Osho has brought a proper understanding to the use of meditation and the whole science of how the techniques are put together.

"In this reviewer's opinion, Rajneesh hits the bull's eye with his emphasis that the 'master key is witnessing: a simple but profound state of watching and accepting ourselves as we are.'

"Rajneesh is an eloquent advocate of meditation. Words such as these have been a genuine source of inspiration."
Meditation, U.S.A.

THE RAJNEESH BIBLE, Vols. 1 - 4

In these talks given in America Osho examines brick by brick the edifice constructed by almost 2000 years of Christianity – its beliefs, its underlying psychology, and its profound influence on the social and political life of modern man. Richly embroidered with hilarious personal anecdotes and statements that shocked even his own disciples, these volumes make it clear why Osho has become the nemesis of established religious and political hierarchies all over the world.

"People say that I am brainwashing people. No, I am not brainwashing people. I am certainly washing their brains – and I believe in dry cleaning!"

"Having spent some of the most memorable hours of my life in his commune at Rajneeshpuram, I know one thing – just one thing – that I will perhaps never again experience anything like that. I don't know anything about religion or faith. Nor am I interested overmuch in such things. But what I saw in Rajneeshpuram is possibly the closest I will ever get to the spiritual experience.

"Any civilization that can produce a man like Osho, even once in a century, has nothing to be ashamed of. And, yes, read these books."

Pritish Nandy, *The Illustrated Weekly of India*

Major Distribution Centers for the works of Osho

EUROPE

Italy
News Services Corporation
Via XX Settembre 12
28041 Arona (NO)
Tel. 02/839 2194
(Milan office)
Fax 02/832 3683

Netherlands
Rajneesh Publikaties
Nederland
Vianenstraat 48
1106 DD Amsterdam
Tel. 020/969 372
Fax 020/890 241

West Germany
The Rebel Publishing
House GmbH°
Venloer Strasse 5-7
5000 Cologne 1
Tel. 0221/574 0742
Fax 0221/523 930

AUSTRALIA
Osho Meditation &
Healing Centre
P.O. Box 1097
Fremantle, WA 6160
Tel. 09/430 4047
Fax 09/384 2822 c/o Raymond

AMERICA

United States
Chidvilas
P.O. Box 17550
Boulder, CO 80308
Tel. 303/449 7811
Fax 303/449 7099
Order Dept. 800/777 7743

Osho Viha Meditation Center
P.O. Box 352
Mill Valley, CA 94942
Tel. 415/381 9861

Also available in bookstores
nationwide at Walden Books

Canada
Publications Rajneesh
P.O. Box 331
Outremont, QUE. H2V 4N1
Tel. 514/276 2680

ASIA

India
Sadhana Foundation°
17 Koregaon Park
Poona 411 001, MS
Tel. 0212/660 963
Fax 0212/664 181

°All books available at cost price